Beautiful. Valuable. Beloved.

AN ANTHOLOGY

Women of Worth

Women of Worth
An Anthology

Cover design by: GreeneHouse Media

ISBN: 978-0-9981690-1-9
Printed in the USA

Published by
FIG Publishing
1500 Beville Road, #606 394
Daytona Beach, Florida 32114
www.FIGPublishing.com
info@FIGPublishing.com

The Value in You

Value is intrinsic
In other words, you were born with it
The space and time you occupy will pay you your dividend,
depending on how you spend it
Your worth on earth is heaven sent
Divine in nature
Through the stages and phases of life we all experience strife
Only the worthy look for the adventure in adversity
Only the noble can turn a catastrophe into currency
So when they told you "You can't do that, please be sensible."
You went out and showed the naysayers that you are somewhat
invincible
Give yourself credit when credit is due
Give the Creator a round of applause because He did an amazing job
when He made you
You've had worth since your birth
You've got glory in your story
You've pushed through the pain to get to the progress, and now
there's no need to worry
Tough times don't last
Tough people do
When the world needs an example of divine perseverance...
they need only to look at you

KNOW YOUR WORTH

~ Mel Roberson
www.MelRoberson.com

Dedication

Women of Worth, an Anthology is dedicated to women around the world who know there is more to who they are than what they have been living. Not everything you've been told about yourself is necessarily true. This book will speak life over you. Here is to your journey of identifying your God-given worth.

"A good woman is hard to find, and worth far more than diamonds."
Proverbs 31:10

Acknowledgements

In preparation of this work, which will bless many around the world, we are grateful for the inspiration, wisdom, and experiences shared by great men and women, including, but not limited to the following:

Project Chaplain -- Dr. Daniel E. Haupt, Sr. You have labored tirelessly in prayer and fasting with and for us. We thank God for the special anointing He has placed upon *Women of Worth, an Anthology* as a result. We appreciate all you have taught us and know that there will be a performance of those things spoken, and not yet seen. We pray a hundred-fold return on all you have sown.

Roundtable Leadership -- Dr. Evelyn Bethune, Jai A. Darden, Ryan C. Greene, Dr. Shirley Clark, and Dr. Stan Harris. Thank you for making yourself available to support and see this project through. Your expertise has moved this idea from vision to an amazing work of healing and inspiration.

Contributing Authors -- Your tireless efforts to fight through the writing and editing processes have not gone unnoticed. Your sacrifices to overcome the potential negative outcomes of the stories you share in this book are the reason this project came to fruition. Know that we are just getting started and the best is yet to come!

You -- Thank you for purchasing this book. We look forward to hearing amazing testimonies as you share with us how your life has been impacted by the stories shared in this work.

Because of the enormity of this project, we may have left out the names of some who contributed along the way. If so, we apologize. Please know that we appreciate you very much.

www.WomenofWorthAnthology.com
E-Mail: Info@WomenofWorthAnthology.com
Facebook: @WomenofWorthAnthology

How to Use this Book

Who is a woman of worth? She seems to be a figment of our imagination, only existing in popular songs, poems and Bible verses. Who could hold such a title in society today? Surely with all we encounter as women, we can't know her personally nor could we possibly be her. Nothing could be further from the truth. Whether you know it or not, you are her. You are that woman of worth; a woman of great value.

This book is written to help you to get a clear understanding of who you are, and whose you are, so you will truly understand your worth … your value! Upon reading these stories, you will gain a greater clarity of your assigned worth based on your Creator and your inherent worth and based on what you have and will create.

We encourage you to read this book with your journal in hand. Take notes on those stories that impact you the most. Connect with the author's vision. If you need a speaker for an event, you have a book full of women and men from which to choose. Need a coach? Our contact information is here for you as well.

It is our prayer and Holy Spirit's promise that as you read, God will speak to you through the pages of this book. You will experience healing and revelation enabling you to live on purpose and find your destiny. Be sure to visit us at www.WomenofWorthAnthology.com and our Facebook page @WomenofWorthAnthology. We wish you more blessings!

Dr. Katrina Ferguson

Table of Contents

Dr. Daniel E. Haupt

FOREWORD

Proverbs 31:10 "Who can find a virtuous woman? for her price is far above rubies."

Women of Worth, an Anthology is a synergistic, prophetic, and inspirational work of literature that reveals to a new generation who she is in the Song of Solomon 8:5 (KJV), the woman who is coming out of the wilderness of her life journey, stimulated to act on destiny and leaning on the arms of her Lover.

The essence of this work reminds me of an adage from our neighbor that unwise guys, who had an immature and uninformed understanding of the worth of the women in their lives, would say: "I don't want your money or your honey. I just want your mind because if I have your mind, you will give me your honey and your money." These guys thought they could possess the assets of a woman's worth through manipulation of the wrong kind of love. Many in today's generation, who have lost the understanding of a woman's true currency of worth need this book, *Women of Worth,* and the substance of hope it provides women to realize their true destiny.

The contributors of this epistle of love are women, handpicked by God, whose souls have been won by the bishop and the true lover of their souls, with the kind of love that caused Him to die for them, and to rise for them, to have their best life. These women have given their lives and their minds to Him whose arm they have learned to lean on. They realize God's goodness and unfailing love that is worthy of the true worth of a woman, who is not just a natural woman but the woman who belongs to God.

With wisdom and precepts, the contributors of *Women of Worth* are prophetic lifelong destiny investigators. They are publishing the true revelation of a woman's worth for a new millennium to discover the identity and true value of God's woman and her value to earth and the heavenlies. *Women of Worth* teaches us that there are women whose vision and destinies are a direct route, but not a straight line. Their insights reveal how with God, they managed and transformed what appeared to be a direct route to destiny, to a disguised reroute. At times their destinies were actually severe mercies to position them to be, do and have what God had always intended for them—to be in position, power and influence.

Women of Worth tells us about the God of Sarah, who was also the God of Hagar, who was in an unfair and unequal situation. Hagar faced what looked like a reroute into direct routes of destiny.

This is not a book for women who want to be ordinary but for women who are ready for a destiny ride to a place I call north of average. After this reading you will not be the same. You will be inspired to realize and manifest your true worth as a woman. This company of women are chosen by God to reveal the woman in Song of Solomon 8:5, who is coming out of her wilderness and into the reality of her promised land. They will give you the inspiration for your divine 'next' and connect you with women whose stories inspire you to fulfill your purpose.

Women of Worth crystalizes that God's woman not only knows God, she knows where she is going in life; to do exploits for the One whose arm she leans on for everything. She inspires others to trust and lean on Him also.

Proverbs 31:29 "Many women do noble things, but you surpass them all."

Foreword

Truly, you must read this 21st century work for men and women to activate and pursue the destiny and worth of the woman who belongs to God—spirit, soul and body.

Dr. Daniel E. Haupt, Sr.

Dr. Daniel E. Haupt, Sr., Dr. Min. and E.D.
7 Mountain Thought Leader, Host of the *Voice of Destiny Show*
Founder of DLINORTH.ORG
www.VoiceofDestiny.org

Dr. Katrina Ferguson

"WOMEN OF WORTH, an Anthology"

Who or what have you allowed to define and determine your worth? What has infiltrated your life and affected the way you view your value and contribution to the world? When you analyze the way you see yourself, you will understand why you behave the way you do. We have allowed others to influence our self-worth to the point that we have no idea who we are, whose we are, or what makes us great. The Amazon bestselling book, *The Queens' Legacy*, tells us "God created women heavenly, and spiritually equipped us with everything that we need. We are daughters of God and that makes us queens." It's our birthright. No matter the circumstance or situation we are facing, we are royalty. Royalty. The very word creates visions of grandeur in our minds and it should. Our price is far above rubies (Prov. 31:10, KJV). That's who we are; that's who you are. Herein lies our value.

We must learn to accept and operate based on our 'inherent' value. Dictionary.com defines inherent as "existing in someone or something as a permanent and inseparable element, quality, or attribute." This is the actual value we possess, rather than the images we are bombarded with on a daily basis through the media and just plain being out and about. These images represent our 'assigned' value. This is value assigned by others and accepted by the masses as cultural, trendy, or even generational choices. Actually, these are indications that we have lost track of our value based on who we are and whose we are.

The media isn't the only source that influences the value we place on ourselves. We often allow well-meaning friends and family to put their price tag on our forehead and we then live based on that falsely assigned value. We cannot allow our value to be colored by anyone, least of all those closest to us. The realization that people can only love you to the extent that they have experienced love, or love themselves, is an indication they will not value you anymore than they value themselves. If they are operating in a place of self-loathing or if they lack self-confidence and self-esteem, they can only give you what they have. This is not a good place to look for validation of your value.

Any reasonable person looking to appraise the value of a thing, looks first to its creator. In our case, this is the only way to measure our worth. By creator, I don't mean our parents. Although my mother loved me more than life itself, it was through her death that I realized she was not able to fully establish within me the depth of my value. Only my Creator could do that. Without minimizing the role of our parents, we only come through our parents; we don't belong to our parents. God had a purpose for our spirit to be in the earth realm and chose our parents to make it happen. Be very careful when you start saying hateful things about them. They were chosen by God to bring you into this world without any regard for the circumstances surrounding your birth. (And we know that all things work together for good to them that love God, to them who are called according to his purpose. Rom. 8:28). Although my mother did everything she knew to do, only God could help me to understand and embrace the value He bestowed upon me.

My teenage years were wrought with challenges because I did not understand my value. Even though there was family who loved me, and friends who surrounded us, they were not able to help. Living in a single parent household, without the daily influence of my father, created a foundation of making decisions based on the holes in the tapestry of my soul. Holes because a crucial piece of the puzzle was missing. My parents divorced and as a result, rarely did I see my father. There were times my mom would say he was coming to pick me up and he did not show. Father-daughter dances with no father. Living only 25 minutes away, my deduction was that he didn't come around because I wasn't good enough or valuable enough for him to be a part of my life. In actuality, the only time I even heard from my father was if Mom called him because I had done something wrong. Without a father to tell me I was beautiful; to tell me I was smart; to tell me I was a gift to the world; and to remind me that in any and every relationship, I was the prize, I believed the opposite.

Not having my father to validate my worth and value meant I would endure a lot of unhealthy relationships, and consequently, a lot of pain, as I attempted to find that value in other men. While my fear of God (at that time the only relationship I had with Him) kept me from falling into sexual promiscuity, it didn't stop me from seeking validation. It was a balancing act between determining value and avoiding fornication. Rather than pray, I became the prey. The prey of every male that crossed my path. It's as if my lack of understanding my value was a magnet, attracting every unsavory voice to speak against my God-given value. Right. It was confusing for me, too.

To add to the difficulty of discovering my value, I was bullied throughout my school experience. Even though Mom worked two jobs most of my life, she placed value on the new house and cars, but we didn't always have the newest of clothes in our closets. Sometimes she even made my clothes. I still remember the kids teasing me saying, "God help what she's wearing," or "hey Roach, make sure you stay out from in front of the bus, cause if you fall, the driver will run over you … you're so black you blend in with the pavement." This was just the beginning of a self-esteem problem that followed me throughout my entire young adult life. (Side note: when I was in school, bullying consisted of saying mean things to people. Today you can literally be bullied to death. Bullying is very serious and something we want to pay close attention to as we raise our children in this generation.)

As a result, much of my time was spent alone. Mom worked to pay for a lifestyle that paralleled what was abandoned when my parents divorced. Dad was absent and there were few, if any friends to be around. This lifestyle didn't allow for much of a social life or involvement with other people for me. The food, for both sustenance and emotional growth, was not readily available and as a result, I learned to depend on myself for validation, companionship, and most everything else. So much so that at times, it was and still can be difficult for me to be around other people for long periods of time.

Eventually, I was introduced to a relationship with Christ and started the journey of coming into the knowledge of Him as my Creator, Savior, and Lord. This is when I started to realize, the formula I was using to calculate my value was all wrong. Much like math in school, it just didn't add up. For years I had been looking to impostors and inventors to assist me in assigning value to my life when all along, the work had been done. Some would say rather than looking to the Creator for my value, I looked to the objects of His creation to find my value.

At some point, I can't even tell you when, I got the idea that my value had nothing to do with people and everything to do with God. With a Bible and a notebook, I set out on a journey of not self-discovery, but God-discovery. As my Creator, I wanted to know what He said about me and what His plan was for my life. I searched and researched the Scriptures to find out what the Creator said about His creation. It seemed that what He said was in direct contradiction with what I believed about myself based on what I had been told and experienced. It was time to embrace a new belief system. Just a few things I learned:

+ I was created in the image of God Himself! ("So God created man in his own image, in the image of God created he him; male and female created he them." Gen. 1:27)

+ God made me good with no qualifiers! ("And God saw everything that he had made, and, behold, it was very good." Gen. 1:31)

+ He knew me and has had a plan for me since before I was born! ("For thou hast possessed my reins: thou hast covered me in my mother's womb. I will praise thee; for I am fearfully and wonderfully made: marvelous are thy works; and that my soul knoweth right well." Psa. 139:13-14)

+ I am beautiful without a flaw! ("You are altogether beautiful, my darling; there is no flaw in you." Song of Solomon 4:7)

The list goes on and on. The revelation that I was a made in His image was the catalyst I needed to help me understand my true value! I continued to go through the Scriptures and began to realize I was not created by accident. God has a purpose for my spirit to be on the earth and He chose my parents to make it happen. Our parents were chosen by God to bring us into this world, regardless of the circumstances surrounding our birth. His plan for our lives speaks directly to our value and purpose.

You may be thinking, well that's good for you. You don't get my situation. I don't have to. Only God does. If you are lacking self-confidence, try God-confidence. Forget about self-esteem, build your God-esteem. If in fact our Creator, God Himself, who breathed His life into us created us in his image as joint heirs with Christ, why in the world would we look to anyone else to ascertain our value? Why do we allow anyone else to speak words of defeat or words of destruction, and not just physical destruction, the destruction that happens on the inside that colors the way you see every situation in your life? Why do we allow people who did not create us to invent a value for us when all we have to do is receive and believe what God has already said about us?

I'll tell you why. It's because no one has sat us down and showed us what God said about us in His Word. We haven't embraced the fact that there is very real purpose for being on this earth. You have a WHY ... a BIG WHY. Visit my YouTube channel and watch the videos so you can be clear about WHY you were created. Once you get this down, you will realize that no matter what you face in life, "If your WHY is BIG enough, the HOW will take care of itself." You can do anything you choose because of who lives inside of you.

Unfortunately, some will not even consider these writings true. Instead, they look for the answers in the latest personal development book. It won't be enough. I'm not putting down personal development. If you know me, you know that I am a personal development fiend. In your process of developing personally, it is imperative that you include the words from your Creator in your study. The Bible gives us principles that are effective regardless of what you believe. If you only operate based on the principles, you are operating in your natural strength. When you accept Jesus as your Lord and Savior, and the Bible as your manual for living, you put His 'super' on top of your natural and possess the ability to see yourself the way God sees you— victorious, confident, whole, and nothing lacking. Take dominion over your life's situations and walk in your complete inheritance as a child of God. Visit our FB group page, click on 'Files' and read, out loud, the prayer of salvation. Be sure to leave us a post that you have joined our family so we can welcome you!

This is a powerful revelation … now. As I matured, I didn't sound anything like this. Because I spent so much time alone, I began to really like myself and became shy; painfully shy. However, no man or woman is an island. We were not created to live life alone. We are created to be social. If you see where I'm going, you realize this in itself is a very difficult thing to do—to love being by yourself and to socialize. A lot of times people don't believe me when I tell them how shy I really am. They see me in videos, on stages, even in pulpits and think there's no way I could be shy. "How can she be in front of all those people. I could never do what she does." These are the very same things I said about myself many years ago. Ironically, it's true. I am extremely shy and introverted. There are times when I am in my home and not see or seek out another person for days, sometimes weeks. I am not the social butterfly I appear to be. Actually, I am probably the most extroverted introvert you'll ever meet. I love people and I love spending time with people—sometimes. More often than not, I prefer to be with a person or two, or all alone, especially after being around great crowds, I need quiet, unstimulated time. I have to retreat into myself or find a place where I can recover and recharge. Thankfully, my closest friends recognize this and don't take offense at my 'cocooning strategy.'

Some say that cocooning is the attribute of a strong person. I say it is the attribute of a person who is prone to insecurity and hasn't fully embraced their worth and value to the world and the universe at large. I had to accept the fact that shyness did not serve me. It did nothing to help me in my pursuit of destiny and purpose. When I fell in love with Jesus in a way that He became Lord, all I wanted to do was to be all He created me to be. This meant shy had to fall away in favor of sacrifices for others, which meant that there was a lot of work for me to do. I had to discover that there was someone other than those mean kids, the rude adults, or the BMW salesman who told me I would never have a nice car. I had to get past all the lies and comments that had nothing to do with who I really was.

When you're clear about the value God has given you, you'll want to be around more people so you can allow your gifting to flow through you to them. I didn't desire to be an inspirational speaker. Inspiration is defined as giving people the hope they need to tap into their true potential and understand their value. I just fell into it. After being involved as a trainer, or having conversations with people, I realized that what I said had a major impact on those involved. Not so much the words, but what was behind them. I could be training on any topic and afterwards people would come and ask me to pray for them. I didn't desire a doctorate or any of the other accolades I carry today. Although I am grateful to God for His favor, it was never my goal to live my life this way. However, I have a goal of obedience to do what God tells me to do.

Understanding your value is not a magic pill against everything that people will say or accuse you of. Assaults to your character and integrity will still come against you to remind you that it's not what happens to you but how you respond to it that matters. There are times when you know you can take someone in an argument, but the Spirit will tell you to hold your peace. You will have to make and take a stand many times during your walk with God. Make sure those stands are based on Him and not on what just happened to you. This is part of the reason why it is so important to determine why you were created in the first place. It's important to know what God's plan is for your life in order to become who He created you to be.

Here you are today, victorious even though you may not feel like it at the moment. We could stay on this path for an inordinate amount of time. Just stop and think of all the things that had to go right for you to sit here reading this story. Maybe everything in your life is not perfect, but God has a plan for your life. You are important. You matter to Him.

About Dr. Katrina Ferguson

In an instant, priorities can shift. As a

- Radio Personality
- Motivator
- Mentor
- Chaplain
- Professional Speaker

- Serial Entrepreneur
- Author
- Trainer
- Life Coach
- And more

Katrina Ferguson delivers a passionate, enthusiastic and entertaining message to teach and encourage you to celebrate your individuality and break through to become your 'greater self.' Her inspiring message is based upon lessons learned in her own breakthrough journeys. Ms. Ferguson is committed to helping others across the world apply these principles in their individual lives and relationships. In her unique, uncompromising style, she brings life-changing principles and leadership skills that have inspired and motivated thousands across age, gender and industry lines. As such, Ms. Ferguson has been the subject of numerous articles and interviews and her story is currently used across the country to train and motivate salesforces of both public and private organizations.

Ms. Ferguson's acute understanding and ability to motivate people has enabled her to excel in the network marketing industry. Her keen awareness that conflicting demands, resource constraints, and shifting priorities are challenges that must be overcome for success in today's global marketplace has placed her in constant demand as a presenter, motivator, and trainer of trainers by sales organizations across the nation.

Ms. Ferguson encourages everyone to be passionate and uncompromising in giving back to the community and celebrating their ability do so. She is chaplain for the WNBA Washington Mystics and the founder and president of A Sister's Love, a nonprofit organization whose mission is to provide practical information, and tangible and intangible tools to assist women and children in achieving while propelling them into greatness.

For more information, to purchase Ms. Ferguson's materials, or to request an appearance, please visit her website at www.KatrinaFerguson.com or email Katrina@KatrinaFerguson.com. Follow her on IG and Facebook @DrKatrinaSpeaks.

Brittany Hampton

Escape to Myself

From a young age, I believed I was a hidden away princess ... until I discovered who I really was. My real parents were rulers of a faraway nation who hid me away until the day I was old enough to discover my true identity and assume the responsibility of my throne. There were even secret spies who followed me everywhere to protect me while on this journey. Many people around me knew my true identity and fought to make sure the wrong people didn't get their hands on me physically or spiritually. My parents here on earth did not even know my true identity, but loved, guided, and fiercely protected me from harm.

This childhood fairytale was not far from the truth.

My journey to discovering my true identity and my worth began when I entered college. Sam Houston State University was my school of choice. Although I had the grades and extracurricular resume to attend any other large school in Texas, something kept drawing me to the small town, southern charm of this university. During my freshman year, I fell into a rhythm of school, volunteer work, and hanging out with newfound friends. I was living the life! No bills to worry about, always having someone to hang out with or an event to attend. I was also part of the freshman leadership group, a collection of high-achieving students from all over the state of Texas. Finally, I had found my 'clique', a group of young leaders in their respective hometowns, like me. A few of us grew close and eventually decided to move off campus together for our sophomore year. We were so excited as we moved our items into our new apartment. New adventures and memories were swirling in our heads and we knew the best times were still ahead.

It was during this time that questions about my future and what I wanted to do after graduation started coming to mind. I had selected a public relations major, but was this what I wanted to do the rest of my life? Many of my choices up to this point came into question and I started to doubt the path I had chosen for myself. What if I was wrong? What if this isn't my purpose? What if I chose the wrong career, or worse, the wrong college? So, amongst all this mental turmoil, I decided I would make some changes. The first one? Dumping my boyfriend of three years. Although I cared about him deeply, I felt it was time to explore the college life without being tied down. I wanted to be free to date and hang out with whomever I wanted. So, while on his way to see me, driving from Dallas to Huntsville, I broke up with him over the phone. Needless to say, he was devastated and didn't take the news very well. I was determined this would be one of the many changes I would implement. But instead of changes for the better, this one decision snowballed me onto a path that I would have never seen myself on.

Fall of my sophomore year saw me partying, drinking in excess, and going home with different guys every week. Homecoming 2010 was one for the ages, but I don't remember much from that week. The most vivid memory was walking into astrology class late, having to sit in the front row, and pulling out my book only to find that my underwear from the night before were stuck in between the pages! I was a wreck. As the semester dwindled down, so did my grades and the decent GPA I had been so proud of. Anxiety and depression took over even further as my roommates were selected to be a part of various sororities and I was not. Our tight knit group was growing apart and I didn't know how to handle it. Something internally kept telling me to push ahead and finish what I started, even if I wasn't sure it was what I wanted.

This is where I was most vulnerable, and also when a brilliant, poetic, dark-skinned gentlemen with dreadlocks entered my life. We met at the first day of my new job at the school newspaper. We talked for hours about our dreams, goals, and life aspirations. He seemed like an amazing guy and I fell for him … fast and hard. A few months into our friendship, he invited me to a church he had been attending in Houston. He said it was a five-fold ministry and that the prophet of the house was truly anointed. These words were foreign to me, but I jumped at the opportunity to hang out with the man I was crushing on. I didn't grow up in church, but I have always believed in God. I always knew that NOTHING ever happened without a reason.

Although the church was sixty miles away from campus, I braved the unseasonably rainy weather that February to meet him in time for the midweek service. The church was filled with sweeping red drapery as powerful worship flowed from the stage in front of a packed house. As I walked in, a young woman greeted me with warmth and kindness while leading me to a seat. All the anxiety I felt about meeting with my future boyfriend, the worries about school, and where my life would go melted away. Looking back on that initial service, that was where I experienced the peace that passed all understanding. As the service progressed, the pastor of the ministry came forth to preach. Just as my friend had said, the man of God was anointed. Everything he spoke about in the service seemed to pertain to some part of my life. For the first time, I felt a sense of knowing, purpose, and direction. I was HYPE. Before the end of the service, the atmosphere shifted, and the prophet felt called to give personal words of prophecy. He called me out of the audience and spoke about funding for schooling that I was lacking (because of my grades) and laid out the vision of God for my life. At that moment I was floored. How could he know about my schooling issues? Does God really speak to people like this? Now I know He does in Amos 3:7: "God does nothing without first telling his prophets." This one encounter with prophecy and the Holy Spirit propelled me into the next season of my life.

From that day, I attended the ministry a few times a week. I wanted to experience the same peace and joy from that first moment I attended. Over the next few months, I learned more about myself, my faults, and how to correct some of the bad thinking that had gotten me in the situation I was in. As we drew closer to the end of the semester, the prophet declared that God was calling me to be a part of the leadership team, a part of those who assisted him in the vision God had given him. I was so excited for the chance to sit under his leadership and learn even more about the things of the Spirit. After service I was invited back to the prophet's office, where all the leadership meetings were held. I sat in the back and listened as the other leaders spoke about the service, the words of prophecy that came forth, and the direction of the ministry. While one of the men was speaking, a young lady entered the room, walked up the prophet, and whispered something in his ear. She also gave him a piece of paper and he looked down and studied it for a bit as the man was finishing up his comment.

He then stood up and said, "Leaders, we have only raised half of what we need to cover the responsibilities of the ministry tonight. How can God trust you with funds for your own home, if you cannot make sure the needs of the house of God are taken care of? Some of you could have given more, but you are holding back. If that is you, I need you to release that seed now!" Needless to say, I was shocked at how his demeanor had shifted in a matter of seconds. He began to speak about how our house is laying in waste because we do not take care of the man of God! "Why do you think so many of you are struggling? Because the man of God is struggling! If I have a roof over my head, don't you think God would provide for you as well?"

He backed his statements up with scriptures and biblical principles concerning sowing and reaping. At the end of his tirade, he said the man of God is leaving, and this church will not be blessed until the man of God and his family were taken care of. He retrieved his Bible and other items, got up, and walked out. This pattern would repeat itself throughout my time in this ministry. The leadership team would regularly have to scramble funds together to appease the man of God, for fear that the Lord would punish us.

We would fundraise until we could not stand any longer. Bake sales, fish frys, and even standing in front of grocery stores and businesses to ask people for money for the ministry. What turned into wanting to follow biblical principles, turned into fear that we would be cursed. The ministry fell into a terrible cycle that summer. We would have powerful services, but not have enough funds to keep the lights on or pay the rent on our building. Leadership meetings would last after service until 1 a.m. We were also expected to be at church almost seven days a week and told that anything that pulled us away was the devil. In that season so many of us lost so much. One leader drained her retirement to take care of the man of God. Another used her rent money and ended up being evicted. Some took out multiple payday loans just to meet their pledges and keep from being 'judged by the Lord' for not taking care of the church. These were not acts done out of the kindness of our hearts, these acts were done out of fear. I ended up giving away my scholarship money and even embezzled funds from a student organization to give a seed to the prophet.

In the span of one summer, I gave more than $10,000 to the ministry. I stopped communicating with my family and friends because they couldn't understand the calling on my life. Whenever someone would say something bad about the prophet, I would cut them off. In my eyes, this man could do no wrong. They were the ones that were flawed and couldn't get it right.

My parents noticed a drastic shift in my behavior that summer. Not only had I stopped talking to my entire family, I even said they were going to be judged for coming against His anointed when they spoke out against the church. My father, along with my grandmother and stepmom, decided to fly from the east coast to check on me. Without informing me they showed up at a Sunday service. I turned around and saw them sitting a few rows back. At that moment, my heart sank and my mind began to race. What were they thinking? Were they going to cause a scene?

After the service, my father embraced me in a hug, and asked if he could have a meeting with the prophet. I tried to make up an excuse that he was too busy and wouldn't have time, but when I made my request known to the leadership team, the prophet accepted. To my surprise, my father calmly stated the reason for coming to see about his daughter and his concerns. To this day, I believe the prophet was so calm because he had met his match. He knew my father had a background in law enforcement and wouldn't dare cross someone of that caliber when he had skeletons in his own closet. After the meeting, my parents drove me back to my university and took away my car, partly because I had mistreated it running up and down the road to church and ultimately to make sure I didn't have a way to get back to the ministry.

Where there's a will, there's a way. I found a way back to the church and for the next four years continued to sit under the cult-like influence of the prophet. My whole life revolved around picking up his children, raising seed to pay his mortgage and car note, and keeping the lights on in the church. All of us were being used for any selfish desires he manipulated us into believing to be God's will.

God will challenge you in certain areas of your life. He will lead you and guide you when those moments occur. This place I found myself in was not God's best for me. After almost four years, I hit my low point. I had been evicted from my apartment twice, slept in various places on campus, at friend's homes, and even in vehicles. I was no longer enrolled in school but spent every waking moment anticipating the instructions of the prophet. I destroyed relationships with my friends and family because of my extreme devotion to this man. There was even a point I stood in front of a trash compactor outside of an apartment, trying to figure out how to throw myself in. I felt like I was spinning my wheels trying to please God. He said He would give me the desires of my heart. Why weren't those things manifesting in my life?

The night I contemplated suicide was a turning point. I had to make changes because I could never go that low again. Instead of going to church in Houston, I began hanging around some of the students in campus ministry, with a group called Daughters of Righteousness

(D.O.R). Although they don't know it, many of these women poured into me during one of the toughest seasons I have walked through. I had been brainwashed and taught that my only worth was to serve the prophet. The ladies of D.O.R. taught me that my worth was in Christ alone, not a church building or in the eyes of a man. Everything I do is important in our Father's eyes. He cares for the sparrow, so how much more would he care for his princess? After almost four years of being a part of that ministry, I gained the courage to pack all my bags and leave Houston. God would never want me to be tormented mentally as I had; and I knew in my heart I needed to make a change if my life was going to get any better. I heard that I was fearfully and wonderfully made. I heard that God had a plan for me. I heard that goodness and mercy would follow me all the days of my life. While I was driving up Highway 45 out of Huntsville, Texas, I knew the truth of my identity had been hidden from me long enough. No matter what was ahead of me, I finally knew who I was in Christ and felt ready to walk into the next season of my life. I finally understood I was the daughter of a King and this princess was finally ready to assume her throne here on earth.

About the Author

Brittany L. Hampton was born in Bethesda, Maryland, on September 1, 1989. At the age of 4, her parents separated. Her mother made the tough decision to move Brittany and her sister to the great state of Texas, where Brittany spent the next twenty years. Brittany is a proud graduate of Duncanville High School in Duncanville, Texas.

After starting her academic career at Sam Houston State University in Huntsville, Texas, Brittany knew she was destined for greatness. But like many young adults, her focus was drawn away to another path that would lead her through a journey that she never imagined. A nondenominational church she joined during her sophomore year turned out to be a cult in disguise. Mentally abusive and manipulative leadership stripped Brittany down to the core of her being. At one point she was homeless, depressed, and even considered suicide. By the grace of God and with the love of her family behind her, she was able to escape the organization and relocate to the Washington, D.C. metro area.

Brittany is currently pursuing a Bachelor of Arts degree in communication studies at The University of Maryland-University College. Her expertise is in relocation and property management, and she finds joy in helping others find and settle into a safe and affordable place they can call home. Brittany is also passionate about helping other young women through telling her story of finding God in a dark time in her life and fighting to be everything she was called to become.

For more information, contact Brittany at Bri.L.hampton@gmail.com and follow her on Instagram @justsimplybrii or @brimovesdmv or Facebook @Blh015.

Burnette Brown

Defying the Odds

Had I allowed the typical expectations of society to write my life's story I would have never become the woman God intended me to be. According to the world's expectations as a young single mother I wasn't supposed to amount to much. The expectations for an African-American single mother looked something like an uneducated person who earned a low income and was most likely dependent on government assistance, minus the hopes of a decent successful future. The world's expectations according to how my story began looked like poverty. Luckily for me I have never been the type of person to allow the expectations of others to dictate my future, my potential, my reality, or more importantly the plans God had for my life.

Like most people I know, I came from humble beginnings. I didn't have the privilege of being born with a silver spoon in my mouth. I was raised by a single mother who worked multiple jobs trying make ends meet just so she could provide the necessities for her children. As a child, my siblings and I were fortunate enough to have a roof over our heads, food to eat, clothes to wear, and a car that transported us from A to B— that is when there was enough money to put gas in it. Unfortunately, since my mother had to work multiple jobs it left plenty of time for other people, usually family members, to watch me.

By the time I was 11 years old I had been molested by two family members and raped by a neighbor. For any adult, these events would be considered unbearable, horrific, and devastating. For a child they were all of that and life-altering. I was robbed of childhood and became an emotionless young girl, unaware of boundaries, looking for love in all the wrong places. I had no idea what love was or what it was supposed to look like. I had been betrayed by people I thought would protect me from the unforgettable pains they imposed on me. While I was looking for what I thought was love, I stumbled upon a life-changing love I never expected—the birth of my daughter. This little 4 lbs., 5 oz. miracle ignited a flame in my morbid soul. I had been hopelessly going through life waiting for a welcomed death to overcome me. Because of her, I had a reason to live.

Life isn't easy at any age. If it was, everyone would be good at it. But now, at 16 years of age, with a baby, it would be that much harder. In my heart, in my mind, in my soul it didn't matter how hard it would be, the only thing that mattered was the reason why I could not fail. In

1991, the year I became a mother, 3.9 million people between the ages of 16–24 had not completed high school. The number was higher for girls who were pregnant. I did not want to be a part of those statistics. I was destined to be different and determined to defy the odds.

Learning was always something I loved, and school afforded me that opportunity. Becoming a young mother, however, created some very difficult obstacles. One thing I was certain of was that I was not going to be a high school dropout. Options like distant or online learning were not available during the time. Still, I was fortunate to attend a pilot program at my school that allowed a few weeks of home tutoring for young mothers. The challenge was that there was no option to take final exams offsite. I certainly couldn't afford childcare and if there were free childcare programs available, I was unaware of them. Determined not to fail and with no other options, I took my daughter with me to school on exam day. I went to my guidance counselor with hopes of getting some help. I informed my counselor that I did not have a babysitter. I asked if I could take my finals because I did not want to fail the year. I was shocked when she told me she would keep my baby in her office so I could take my exams. As an adult, I often wonder what would have happened had I not had the courage to ask that simple question.

Don't ever miss an opportunity to achieve your goals because you are afraid to ask for help. You may be surprised how many people will support your desire to succeed. I could have easily given up on my education and pursued a GED later in life, but I wanted better for my daughter. I wanted better for myself. That day I passed every single exam. Not only did I graduate from high school, but I doubled up on a few classes and was able to graduate early. In my mind, I had decided that my circumstances would not dictate what I could accomplish or how far I would go in life, I chose to believe that even in the face of my current circumstances, I could accomplish anything I set my mind to. After all, if I didn't believe in myself, who would? Although this one accomplishment did not make life any easier, the experience taught me how to endure the other struggles I would eventually experience in life.

Shortly after finishing high school, I watched as my husband became hooked on cocaine. As the hands of his addiction, I experienced more emotional and physical abuse than I could stand. As soon as opportunity presented itself, I knew I had to escape what could have been a short-lived life. One morning when my husband left for work, I took my daughters and left. With one suitcase filled with whatever clothes I could fit for myself and my daughters, we narrowly escaped with our lives. Now, at the age of 19, my two daughters and I became residents of a women's shelter for domestic violence victims. Fatefully, I would be living in the same room at the shelter that my sister occupied several years prior. This became one of the most humbling experiences of my life. At the shelter I was given a contract that explained the house rules and I was provided with padlocks, one to lock my refrigerator and one to lock my room door. This was not the life I wanted my kids to experience.

Although I had not been a mother very long, I felt like I had already failed my children. My only hope was that when they grew older, they wouldn't remember these events since they were so young. I knew I had to compose a plan to get my life on a more positive track. With only a high school education and no income, I had to endure a setback in order to make a strong comeback in the future. I had to accept government assistance to be able to provide for my myself and my children. I can remember being so embarrassed to use food stamps that I would wait to go grocery shopping in the middle of the night. I knew that this situation was only temporary, yet that did very little to camouflage the embarrassment or shame I was feeling.

There had to be a better way. So, I came up with a plan to avoid a lifetime in the system. My plan included public assistance for five years and then we would be self-sufficient. I am proud to say after five years, I no longer needed it. There is no shame in needing help for a season. We are all human and are not exempt from falling on hard times. Most people are four paychecks away from being in trouble financially. There is, however, something wrong with accepting mediocracy and not exhausting every effort to better your situation. During this process, there were two things I held on to that gave me the strength to keep moving forward. First, I had to be a person that my children could be proud of. Second, I would not allow my children to grow up having to experience what I had to go through. I am proud to say many years later that I succeeded.

Throughout all the challenges I have faced, I never allowed myself to stop believing in my ability to defy the odds and to make the impossible possible. I never stopped believing I could accomplish whatever I set my heart and mind to do. The only person I have ever had to compete with in life was myself. Because I set high expectations for myself, it wasn't always an easy thing. Refusing to give up and deciding to succeed was a daily battle for me. My personal life experiences, both good and bad, prepared me for the woman I needed to be today. In life, it is important that we never lose sight of that. The temporary struggles we face at certain points in life will eventually pass, but the lessons we learn from those struggles and experiences will shape us into the person we need to be in the future.

As you can imagine, as a mother of six beautiful children, life has dished out its share of struggles, heartaches, challenges, and obstacles. I do not regret anything I experienced because they have molded me into the person I am today. During the darkest times in my life, I was angry with God and would often ask Him why I had to endure so much hurt, pain, and disappointment. For years I did not get an answer. Finally, during one of my dimmest moments, as I cried out to God in anger, I asked Him, "why me?" I got the answer I had waited so long for and His answer relieved me of so much resentment that I sheltered inside of me. God very clearly spoke to my spirit revealing that I had to go through it in order to help someone else get through it. In the same way you couldn't explain to someone how good chocolate ice cream tastes if you have never tasted it, you cannot relate, understand, or empathize with anyone if you have not lived through what they are experiencing. At that very moment, it all became worth it, including the hurt, pain, continuous disappointments, and even the sexual assault. If my going through meant that I could be someone else's hope, then it will always be worth it.

Despite our experiences or circumstances, we all have the right to choose. We can choose to allow our situation or circumstances to overtake us and allow those things to stifle our growth, or we can choose to accept our past, learn from our experiences or mistakes, and rewrite a better future. My choice has been and always will be to defy the odds. I pray that your choice will be the same.

About the Author

A native New Yorker, Burnette has called North Carolina her home for 13 years. As a young single mother, Burnette realized the importance and power of higher education. As a lifetime learner, she holds an A.A.S with a concentration in leadership, a B.B.A with a concentration in management and is currently pursuing a Master of Science degree in management while simultaneously obtaining a Certified Associate Project Management Certification (CAPM).

Her most rewarding accomplishments include being a mother to six wonderful children and serving as the founding president of Single Mothers Helping Others, a nonprofit organization where the mission is to assist domestic violence survivors become self-sufficient by offering financial counseling, educational resources, access to temporary shelter, and providing food and clothing resources.

Ms. Brown's passion and purpose is encouraging and motivating young women and single mothers to defy the odds and become the best version of their self by setting attainable goals, incorporating effective life skills, and making personal, physical, and mental self-care a necessity.

For more information or to schedule a speaking engagement, please contact Burnette Brown at BurnetteBrown@ymail.com and momshelp@outlook.com.

Carolyn White-Washington

Woman, You Have Worth

Quietly she sits in the courtroom fidgeting with papers watching the door, fearful for his appearance. Glancing at the clock on the wall and the documents in her lap, she wonders how she ended up in this place. He came into her life like a knight in shining armor on a white horse-drawn carriage. Tall, dark, handsome, retired from the military, successful—all the qualities any woman would long for. Most importantly, he chose her to be his wife. She felt loved, adored and appreciated. Just like her whirlwind romance, everything happened in a flash, and after a few months of marriage, what had been her knight in shining armor became her nightmare from hell as he became abusive, threatening, and violent to the woman he so lovingly promised to cherish for life.

While sitting in the darkened courtroom with no legal representation, she had only the support of me and a couple members of our Sisterhood, Sisters4Sisters, Inc. We sat silently in prayer, waiting for the judge to call her name. As we waited, we witnessed more than twenty cases being dismissed because the plaintiff, the victim, did not appear in court. This resulted in defendants and abusers being released, taken off the hook as their cases were dismissed, one after another, after another. Shockingly, men with extensive records of abuse were being released because their victims did not show up to speak on their own behalf. I left the courtroom that day a changed woman. The pain was overwhelming for those who did not have the strength, the courage, or the voice to share their story, nor to defend their worth.

Each year in the United States more than 1.3 million women are victims of abuse. Many of these victims are in these relationships because they do not feel worthy. As the founder and executive director of Sisters4Sisters, Inc. our mission is to empower women and girls in mind, body and spirit. We are committed to providing a safe, sacred and spiritually stimulating space where sisters can share, succeed, and soar. Since 1999, our focus has been to empower, enrich, enlighten, engage, enhance, and educate women and girls. In the courtroom that day, with one of our beloved members, our mission and our goal was expanded to another dimension.

My purpose for women's empowerment was birthed out of a place of my personal pain. I was bullied in school and treated unfairly by girls throughout elementary and middle school. Although they were unkind to me, even as a young girl, I could see they were in deep conflict and sadness. Instead of retaliating by being mean and bitter, I instead chose to be compassionate and forgiving. This led to my divine purpose in mentoring and encouraging women and girls from all facets of life.

As an empowerment strategist for women and girls, I have observed the unresolved trauma many of us face and carry throughout our journey. It is my prayer that my life will be a light and hope for those who feel misunderstood, isolated, and in search of healing and restoration.

After that courtroom appearance, I created and developed The LOVE (Leave Out Violence Everyday) Movement. The LOVE Movement is dedicated to education, awareness, and providing direct services for survivors of domestic/sexual violence and human sex trafficking.

Many victims of domestic violence do not feel worthy to be loved thus resulting in unhealthy and abusive relationships. No matter how beautifully a woman is dressed or how educated she may appear, domestic violence can impact anyone anywhere. From the gated estate communities of wealth to the urban gated windows of the inner city, domestic violence shows up in all zip codes. One of the major components of The Love Movement is education, which can prevent and eradicate domestic violence.

What Is Domestic Violence?

Domestic violence, also called intimate partner violence (IPV), domestic abuse, or relationship abuse is a pattern of behavior used by one partner to maintain power and control over another partner in an intimate relationship. Domestic violence does not discriminate. Anyone of any race, age, sexual orientation, religion, or gender can be a victim or perpetrator of domestic violence. It can happen to people who are married, living together, or who are dating. It affects people of all socioeconomic backgrounds and education levels.

It's not always easy to tell at the beginning of a relationship if it will become abusive but there are signs that you should be aware of. Many partners appear to be perfect in the early stages of a relationship. Possessive and controlling behaviors don't appear overnight, but rather emerge and intensify as the relationship grows. Domestic violence doesn't look the same in every relationship because every relationship is different. But one thing most abusive relationships have in common is that the abusive partner does things to have more power and control over their partner. Stay alert, pay attention and be aware.

The LOVE Movement educates on various signs and indicators of potential dating violence referred to as the Purple Flags.

They include:

- Hitting, punching, kicking, shoving, choking or slapping
- Calling you out of your name, using excessive profanity
- Using weapons to inflict harm or threaten you

- Controlling what you eat or when you sleep
- Forcing you to do work against your will
- Forcing or pressuring you to use drugs or alcohol
- Stopping you from seeking medical treatment or calling the police
- Attacking your sense of self-worth
- Insulting you, calling you names, criticizing you, humiliating you
- Acting jealous or possessive, accusing you of being with other partners
- Withholding affection or acknowledgement in order to punish you
- Cheating on you
- Lying to you
- Threatening to hurt you, your loved ones, your pets, your children, or your possessions
- Controlling the time you spend with others, or monitoring where you go
- Controlling what you wear, often with the accusation that you attract too much attention
- Damaging or stealing your belongings
- Blaming you for the abuse, saying that you deserve what happens or that you instigated the problem
- Gaslighting: saying things to make you question your perception of reality, such as "That never happened, you never remember correctly"
- Forcing or manipulating you to perform sexual acts

- Demanding sex when you're not willing or able
- Harming you during sex by choking, holding or striking you
- Forcing you to watch pornography
- Insulting you in sexual ways
- Refusing to use a condom or other method of birth control
- Refusing to let you use birth control
- Sabotaging birth control efforts such as poking holes in condoms, swapping out birth control pills, not pulling out, forcibly removing an IUD, etc.
- Forcing you to become pregnant
- Forcing you to have an abortion, or preventing you from getting one, regardless of your wishes
- Preventing you from having access to bank accounts with your money
- Only permitting you to spend from an allowance
- Monitoring how you spend money and deciding what you can or cannot buy
- Stealing your money or using your savings without your permission
- Refusing to contribute to shared expenses such as rent, food, childcare, etc.
- Sending you insulting or threatening messages over text, email or social media
- Using social media sites like Facebook to track what you are doing and where you are
- Demanding you send sexually explicit photos or videos of yourself, or sending you their own

- Looking through your phone and checking your call history, texts, pictures, etc.
- Ordering you to not turn off your phone or punishing you when you don't answer
- Following you
- Spying on you, including cyber stalking
- Sending you unwanted packages, letters, texts, or messages
- Calling you at home or at work after you've told them not to contact you
- Showing extreme jealousy of your friends and time spent away
- Keeping you or discouraging you from seeing friends or family members
- Insulting, demeaning or shaming you with put-downs
- Controlling every penny spent in the household
- Taking your money or refusing to give you money for necessary expenses
- Looking at you or acting in ways that scare you
- Controlling who you see, where you go, or what you do
- Preventing you from making your own decisions
- Tells you that you are a bad parent or threatens to harm or take away your children
- Prevents you from working or attending school
- Destroys your property or threatens to hurt or kill your pets
- Intimidates you with guns, knives or other weapons
- Pressures you to have sex when you don't want to or do things sexually that you're not comfortable with

These are signs and indicators we must begin to discuss and share openly with those in our circle of influence, including women and girls of all ages.

Although they have encountered violence, many victims are often unaware or unable to leave unhealthy and abusive relationships. Statistics show that a victim will leave and return to an abusive relationship seven to nine times before finally leaving. People often wonder why a person won't just leave an abusive relationship. Leaving is often the most dangerous time for a victim of abuse, because abuse is about power and control. When a victim leaves, they are taking control and threatening the abusive partner's power, which could cause the abusive partner to retaliate in very destructive ways.

Aside from this danger, there are many reasons why people stay in abusive relationships. Here are just a few of the common ones:

- **Fear:** A person may be afraid of what will happen if they decide to leave the relationship.

- **Believing Abuse is Normal:** A person may not know what a healthy relationship looks like, perhaps from growing up in an environment where abuse was common, and they may not recognize that their relationship is unhealthy. This can be generational in nature.

- **Fear of Being Outed:** If someone is in an LGBTQ relationship and has not yet come out to everyone, their partner may threaten to reveal this secret.

- **Embarrassment or Shame:** It's often difficult for someone to admit that they've been abused. They may feel they've done something wrong by becoming involved with an abusive partner. They may also worry that their friends and family will judge them.

- **Low Self-Esteem:** When an abusive partner constantly puts someone down and blames them for the abuse, it can be easy for the victim to believe those statements and think the abuse is their fault.

- **Love:** So often, the victim feels love for their abusive partner. They may have children with them and want to maintain their family. Abusive people can often be charming, especially at the beginning of a relationship, and the victim may hope their partner will go back to being that person. They may only want the violence to stop, not for the relationship to end entirely.

- **Cultural/Religious Reasons:** Traditional gender roles supported by someone's culture or religion may influence them to stay rather than end the relationship for fear of bringing shame upon their family.

- **Language Barriers/Immigration Status:** If a person is undocumented, they may fear that reporting the abuse will affect their immigration status. Also, if their first language isn't English, it can be difficult to express the depth of their situation to others.

- **Lack of Money/Resources:** Financial abuse is common, and a victim may be financially dependent on their abusive partner. Without money, access to resources, or a place to go, it can seem impossible for them to leave the relationship. This feeling of helplessness can be especially strong if the person lives with their abusive partner.

- **Disability:** When someone is physically dependent on their abusive partner, they can feel that their well-being is connected to the relationship. This dependency could heavily influence their decision to stay in an abusive relationship.

If you have a friend or family member experiencing domestic violence there are ways you can support them.

Support for Your Abused Loved Ones

It can be difficult to watch someone you care about deal with an abusive relationship. Even more difficult is watching that person leave and return to their partner, time and time again. You might feel frustrated, angry, or you may even feel like giving up on your friend or family member. These are all totally normal and understandable feelings to have.

But it's important to remember that domestic violence is extremely complex. Leaving an abusive relationship is never easy, and it isn't always the safest option. If you find yourself in this role, you might ask yourself what you can do to make sure you are staying helpful and supportive.

Educate Yourself. Understanding the dynamics of domestic violence is important when supporting a person in an abusive relationship. A greater understanding of these dynamics may help you develop more empathy for your friend or family member who is experiencing these things in their relationship.

Let Your Loved One Know You're Concerned. This can be a really difficult conversation to have, but you can start it by simply saying, "I've noticed that your partner says mean things to you/doesn't let you go out as much/puts you down in front of other people, etc., and I'm concerned about those behaviors.

Listen and Support Their Decisions. People in abusive relationships often feel they have little control over their lives. Their abusive partners have taken control, and they may be dependent on them in multiple ways. It can be tough to support a person's decision to return to or stay with their abusive partner but try to avoid telling your friend what they should do.

Encourage Small Steps and Help Them Find Options Specific to Their Needs. There is no one-size-fits-all solution to domestic violence. Many survivors feel overwhelmed by the idea of leaving for good or taking drastic measures such as calling law enforcement, so try to help them identify small steps they can take to feel safer and more empowered and/or move toward.

Practice Self-Care in Helping Others. Secondary trauma is real and very common. Supporting someone in an abusive relationship can take a mental and emotional toll on you. If you find yourself getting frustrated with your friend, it can be a really important time to take a step back and focus on your own self-care.

Remind them that they are worthy and fearfully wonderfully made in the image of God. When leaving and ending an abusive relationship, take time to identify your worth and set a new standard on how you should be treated.

Over the years, The LOVE Movement has developed a program which provides healing services with suggestions for women to journal. Some of the journal topics suggested includes the following:

- To write and identify the qualities which make you feel worthy. Perhaps you are loving, caring, compassionate, giving, etc.

- Jot down these qualities and keep them visible (love those Post-its!!).

- Do a Gratitude Journal – Write down five things daily for which you are grateful.

- Make a list of people who no longer serve your highest good, who make you feel unworthy and then lovingly limit or reduce your time and energy with them.

- What triggers your feelings of self-loathing? Write it down. Now forgive yourself for your humanness (and keep on forgiving yourself).

- Recite daily affirmations. I am beautiful and worthy. I deserve the best in life, and I choose to surround myself with loving, supportive people, thoughts and life experiences.

Without knowing your worth you lack the motivation to be honored and respected like you should be treated. Clearly understanding the *Worth of a Woman* will remind you that you should not be in an abusive, unhealthy relationship, and that you should be treated well because you are worthy of positive and loving life experiences.

You are Worthy! You are Enough! You Matter!

Everyone deserves a relationship that is positive, healthy, and free from domestic violence. If you have concerns about your relationship, you can seek assistance from the following:

The National Domestic Violence Hotline - Hotline advocates are available to help 24/7 at 1-800-799-7233 or via live chat from 7 a.m. to 2 a.m.

Sisters4Sisters, Inc.- The LOVE Movement

Sisters Real Talk- Keeping it 100 About Domestic Violence. Chat with them 24-7 Recorded Chat on Domestic Violence 1-800-283-1194.

Charla Gix

My Mother's Keeper

It was November 23, 1978, at 11:59 p.m. on a cold winter night. I entered this world feet first, "breeched" in medical terms, and have been running backwards ever since, as my mom would say.

At the age of 11, I had to grow up fast. I noticed my mom would go to work, come home, give me money, and go straight to her bedroom and not come out for hours. No dinner was cooked; no conversations to discuss our day. Mind you, I knew my mom would often be tired from working long shifts, but she would still sacrifice and spend time with me and my younger siblings. I also noticed this man would come over to see my mom, mostly on payday. He would walk in and go straight to my mom's bedroom. It was not until later that I realized that man was my mom's drug supplier.

A couple of years went by and I found myself in the mom role to my younger siblings. I can remember having no less than $1,000 to $1,200 in my pocket as a 13-year-old. My mother would say, "Here baby, take this money and take care of what needs to be taken care of around the house." I was also responsible for making sure my younger siblings had what they needed and food to eat. We would walk down the street from the house to the local shopping plaza where there was a Dollar Store, a Sav-A-Lot grocery store, and Sharpe's, a department store across the street. Sharpe's allowed me to charge clothes and shoes on my mother's Georgia-Pacific account where she was employed.

At times I was bitter and angry because I needed my mom during some very important times of my life. Due to her drug addiction, she was not there, most specifically when my menstrual cycle started. I remember that day like it was yesterday. I was 12 years old and had just come in from a softball game. I told my little brother to do something, but he refused. So, I attempted to force him to do it. We started fighting and he kicked me between my legs. I ran to the bathroom in pain and that is when I noticed that there was blood in the seat of my underwear. I called my mother and started telling her about the fight with my brother and how he kicked me between my legs, causing my "pocket book" to start bleeding. After hearing the story, she realized what happened and explained to me that my menstrual cycle had started. I was so confused about the whole situation. After many trials and errors, I figured it out.

As the years passed, my mother's drug addiction got worse and we had to move a lot. My mother lost her job, went to rehab and relapsed. We had to live with my dad a few times. Just a lot! On top of all that, I became pregnant at the age of 15. I didn't even know what was going on. My dad would send me and my younger sibling to basketball camp at Louisiana Tech during the summer months. During one particular summer camp I became sick. I was nauseous, throwing up, could not eat, and was restless.

My dad allowed us to visit my mom sometimes during the summer when he knew she was clean. After camp that summer, he allowed us to stay with my mother. The nausea, vomiting, inability to eat and restlessness continued. Finally, after a couple of weeks of not feeling better, my boyfriend's sister took me to the doctor. That is when I found out I was pregnant. I passed out at the doctor's office in disbelief. My whole life was about to change, and I was not ready. All I could think about was there would be no more basketball, outings with friends, prom or anything else that teenagers enjoy. I received a WIC folder and my next appointment.

Once I arrived back at my mother's house, I placed the WIC folder on the kitchen table and went straight to my bedroom to hibernate. My mind was so heavy. All I could think was either my mom was going to kill me or put me out. When I heard my mom come in the house, I wanted to go hide in the closet. I knew she saw the WIC folder on the table because she was quiet. She called for me to come into the kitchen. I could see her standing up against the wall holding the folder in her hand, with a look of disappointment on her face. She asked me how far along I was and what was my plan with a baby at the age of 15. I had no answers for her. After a couple days she came to me and said we would get through the situation together. I was happy because I did not want my dad to find out I was expecting. Actually, he did not find out until I was seven months pregnant. I thought he was going to have a heart attack. He was disappointed but eventually he came around and excepted the fact that he was going to be a grandfather again.

My first child was born February 4, 1996, while I was a sophomore in high school. After my child was born, I lost friends and basketball opportunities, but most of all my childhood and freedom. I can remember my mom being there for me and doing the best she could for me and my daughter. Once I was old enough, I got my first job at McDonald's. My daughter's dad was not very supportive emotionally or financially. Although it hurt my feelings, I just moved on with my life.

Years passed, I graduated high school, but was unable to start college. I continued to work so I could take care of my daughter and help my mother with the bills. My mother returned to using drugs and eventually moved a couple of her friends in the house with us who also had drug addictions. I was stressed out at this point and worried about leaving my daughter with her to babysit. I knew my mother loved my daughter and would not let anything happen to her. Being under the influence of drugs, I just did not trust her to babysit that often. I remember coming home from work one day and my mother told me my daughter burned her side because she was trying to open the cabinet above the heater in the bathroom. Later, during one of my mother's stays at a rehab facility, she wrote a letter confessing that my daughter walked in the bathroom while she was smoking a crack pipe and reached for the pipe. My mother said she tried to turn away before my daughter reached for it, but she had already grabbed it and dropped it on herself after she realized it was hot. I was so upset after I found this out that I did not speak to my mom for days.

Years, months, weeks and days went by as I watched my mother go in and out of different rehabilitation centers only to relapse shortly after getting out. I used to say she just going to get some rest. She lost houses, cars, jobs, friends, trust, and almost lost her children due to her drug use. She was in and out of jail for writing bad checks. As soon as she would go to jail, I would run myself crazy calling friends and family members to help bond her out. She would miss court and eventually the police would issue a warrant and come right back to pick her up. I would go get her every time until one day I could not.

It was a summer day and my mother took my daughter to the store with her. My uncle and other family members were at our house hanging out and fellowshipping. Everyone was hanging outside. Suddenly, we saw my mother coming down the street driving what appeared to be seventy miles per hour. The police were close behind with flashing lights and blaring sirens. My mother drove into the yard and the police pulled up with guns drawn on my mother. My baby was in the back seat of the car looking confused just like everyone else in the yard. I remember my uncle asking the police what was going on and if it was necessary for them to have their guns drawn. They told my uncle to be quiet. I then stepped between the police officer and my mother and pleaded with the police officer to not shoot my mother. The police stated that they tried to pull my mother over because she had warrants but she would not stop the vehicle. The police finally put their guns away after my mother stopped resisting arrest. She was booked into the county jail with no bond, so this time I could not get her out. She appeared in court about a week later and the judge refused to give her a bond. After going to trial for all the bad checks and resisting arrest, they offered my mother nine years in prison.

My father hired an attorney. Once the attorney became involved with the case and told the judge my mother had a history of drug abuse, he gave my mother six months in the county jail. She was required to complete a six-month drug rehab program and afterward she was placed on probation, which required her to take a drug screen every week. If the drug screen came back positive, she would have to serve those nine years. My mother successfully completed the jail time, rehab and probation without any mess ups. I think having no bond was the best thing that could have happened. My mom has been drug-free for more than twenty years now.

Once I saw my mother was herself, she regained my trust and I began to move on with my life. I enrolled at the University of Louisiana at Monroe and obtained a bachelor's degree in arts and science in 2007. I completed a master's degree in special education in 2011. I always stayed by my mothers' side no matter what. Once they got older, my other siblings moved on with their lives and started families and careers. I am truly my mother's keeper. Even today I live only forty-five minutes from my mother.

Growing up my life was not always easy and a lot of times I was ready to give up on life—period. I thank God for touching my mind and keeping me safe while I went through my trials and tribulations. I do not think I could have picked a better person to go through what I had to go through. This is my testimony to encourage someone that there is hope and light at the end. I always think of the Book of Revelation which shows that in the end we win! I stand and believe that right today. I am a woman and I know and understand my worth. Knowing your worth is so important. Loving yourself first will help you love others despite how they treat you or have treated you.

About the Author

Charla K. Gix was born in Greenville, Mississippi on November 23, 1978. Charla had to be born in Mississippi, because there were no hospitals in her hometown of Portland, Arkansas. She has called Monroe, Louisiana, her home since 2000. Married with four wonderful children, Charla is employed by the Monroe Housing Authority. She works part time at Copeland's of Monroe as a manager, and at The Living Waters Outreach Ministries.

Charla completed a bachelor's degree in arts and science, with a concentration in sociology from the University of Louisiana at Monroe in 2007. She also graduated with a master's degree in special education from Grand Canyon University in 2011. She is currently enrolled at Capella University to obtain a second master's degree in mental health counseling in hopes of obtaining an LPC license.

Charla loves spending time with family, traveling, and meeting new people. She also enjoys helping her community and collaborating with community resources to meet the needs of low- to moderate- income families. Charla also performs a great deal of volunteer work with United Way. She is very active at her church, The Living Gospel of West Monroe, Louisiana. During her down time, she enjoys reading and writing.

To book Charla K. Gix to speak or train at your next event, contact her by email at charlakennedy@hotmail.com.

Ella Coleman

Appreciating Self Value Through Life Experiences

A woman's worth is immeasurable. Her divine design, complexity, and beauty alone are beyond human discovery. She has the authority to oversee her own priceless value, whether she knows it or not. So, it is not so much how others see her but how she sees herself. Self-worth or self-esteem can be an innate revelation for some, a taught preservation for many, a long journey to realization for others, and unfortunately, a fragmented illusion to so many. Whatever a woman's assessment of her personal worth, know that to the One who made her, she is a one-of-a-kind masterpiece. That being said, travel with me on this brief journey of my own self-worth.

As a "southern girl" reared in the Mississippi and Memphis areas, I grew up involved church, school, and visiting relatives. I often wondered why I was born in the poorest state in the United States to descendants of enslaved people. Notice, I said "enslaved" because in my mind, I thought my people were too royal to be slaves and later during historical and family research, I discovered I was right. I was a lofty little girl who considered myself a ruling princess. Others who knew me understood my mindset and many times accommodated it.

In spite of my perceived nobility, home was in a place of humble beginnings, where I lived with my mother and her family. My maternal grandfather and grandmother impacted my life greatly. My grandmother took care of me when Mom went to work. My grandfather, a landscaper and a farmer, worked very hard to support his family, which included the younger of his eight children who were still at home, and some of his grandchildren.

As the first grandchild to live with them, I received extra attention. That love contributed to my self-value. It was a major ingredient in the glue that held me together when I was tried and rejected in the future. This communal environment rooted me in a family love that established my strong self-worth to navigate in colder and harsher places in the north.

Love strengthened me to endure, persevere, and advance in life. Love was my starting point in grasping a balanced perspective for a healthy self-esteem. This is how God prepared me for the forthcoming obstacles that would challenge me without my foreknowledge of what would come.

Going to church was an accepted part of our community culture. How vividly I remember the hymns, the choir, the preaching, the intense prayers, Sunday school, and fellow congregants who were all part of our little southern community of black people in the segregated south. Giving my life to Jesus Christ at age 11 was a momentous occasion. I was put on the "mourners' bench" where mostly tweens—10, 11, and 12-year-olds—were converted and later baptized.

Those were old fashioned nightly revivals. I recall the deep public prayers of the deacons, who prayed over us children to receive salvation. By the second night of one particular revival, I could not resist and in tears I submitted my life to Jesus. Although I didn't understand it all, in my young mind, I knew God valued me and would not send me to hell. To me, that was a great relief and the beginning of a personal spiritual experience with God.

When my mom and stepfather moved to Ohio, I didn't desire to go because I didn't want to leave my friends, school, nor my family members. Interestingly, they allowed me to stay and continue living with my grandparents, who didn't want me to leave, either. Consequently, I enjoyed school years in the South and summers in the North. It was perfect I thought, but a change was coming.

At age 12, I heard God's voice telling me to go and live in Ohio with my parents. I felt God speaking to my heart before but never in an audible voice. I knew I was supposed to relocate. I would turn 13 in

August and school started in early September. I told my parents I would come to Ohio to live and start the 8th grade there. Family members and friends were saddened by the news, but I knew it was what I had to do.

Life in the North was quite different. Unlike East Side High, which was all black, Starling Junior High was integrated. For the first time in my life, I attended a school where sixty percent of the students were white, and the majority of the teachers were white. I quickly acclimated because I made friends while visiting during previous summers and observed that Ohio was not like down home. Prior to moving to Columbus, I never had a white teacher. My black teachers in Mississippi were like parents. They used corporal punishment and talked to us students like we were their sons and daughters. My new teachers weren't like that.

I believe adjusting to a new environment made me stronger and wiser. It was a real-life exercise that taught me to be flexible and to adapt to change without overreacting. This proved to be beneficial in the future. Also, it enabled me to be more secure in less friendly, perhaps somewhat intimidating environments.

High school was another place of development and growth. I was active at Central High School and made many friends. I became a varsity majorette and performed at all our football games with the marching band. Central was the first school in our area to offer computer training and I was in that class. I did office work after school and was happy to receive my first paycheck. Teen life can be

challenging and although I loved to attend parties with my friends, I'm sure my parents were glad I stayed out of trouble.

Still, I was not naïve to the issues affecting the world, particularly my own black community. I remember protesting at the Columbus School Board with a group of fellow students. We demanded that black history be taught in the public schools. I recall local television reporters asking us questions. We responded with one voice, "The revolution will not be televised," which was a popular poem by Gil Scott Heron. Without a doubt, this activism impacted my view of myself and other black people. Our rights were worth fighting for.

The fight in me was advantageous in years to come. There were detours and setbacks along the way because there was much to learn. I was adventurous and ambitious. Normal stuff bored me and normal guys who were interested in dating me, bored me as well. I knew my life was different. I was a visionary and an independent thinker with an upbeat attitude. I worked a while before going to college, which made me realize that a 9 to 5 job was not going to be my ultimate career choice.

I dreamed of so much more, which caused me to join a female vocal group called Sweet Harmony. We practiced a lot after work, and we were very excited when we auditioned to be the background singers for a band headed by one of the original Ohio Players. They chose us for the job, but it never happened because they were severely injured in a terrible vehicular accident before we had a chance to sign the contract. God was letting me know that entertainment wasn't the life He chose for me.

I headed to college in the late 70s, Capital University was another place of great learning and personal growth. I majored in speech communications/broadcasting and minored in professional writing. My class schedule was full, but I enjoyed that small university campus, where I met life-long friends. I also enrolled in a few music courses and learned to play the flute. Opportunities were readily available to feed my ambitious spirit. I received an internship at a major radio station, where I covered and recorded news stories, went to press conferences, and drove a station news car. Soon I found out that some of the white students in my broadcasting class were unhappy and jealous that they weren't chosen for this magnificent internship. I really didn't care what they thought. I was happy. I loved me and knew God opened that door.

In addition, an unusual offer was extended by the head of the Physical Education Department. Even though all students were required to take physical education, when I explained to her that I had my own regimen and practiced yoga, she asked me if I would teach a yoga class. Of course, I said, "Yes!" I was soon teaching yoga for college credit at Capital while I was student.

After graduating, I applied for a news reporter position at one of the local television stations. When I arrived and the interviewer saw that I was a black, he left the office and didn't return. Departing a bit angry, I thought to myself, "I didn't really want that job anyway." Shortly

thereafter, I began working at the local black newspaper, *The Call &
Post*. It seemed like everyone came to *The Call & Post*: preachers,
politicians, teacher, society ladies, etc. It was not what I expected but
I gleaned a lot about publishing. I worked directly with Mr. Amos
Lynch, who was affectionately called "The God Father" because he
was one of the most powerful men in the community. Certainly,
working for him tested me and made me stronger. He talked to me like
I was his daughter instead of an employee. In fact, many times he
called me daughter. Mr. Lynch was old enough to be my father, so I
respected him. He was instrumental in helping me to get my first
passport to visit West Africa. Yet, I knew my worth and accepted an
opportunity to leave for better position.

A new black-owned radio station was coming to town and I was
determined to apply for a position. During the interview, I told them,
"You all need me." They liked my tenacity and hired me on the spot.
I became public affairs director, sold advertising, and hosted "Express
Yourself," the number one talk show in the black community. I
became known for the show and met and interviewed people from all
walks of life during my six years there. The job prepared me for
entrepreneurship because I set my own schedule and earned money as
a salesperson on commission. I was blessed to attend The Ohio State
University and earn a master's degree while working at the station.

Yet, I knew I had to move on. A new vision had been divinely given
to me to start my own magazine, *Purpose*. It was on April Fools' Day,
1991, when God told me, "Today is your last day at the radio station.
Call the owner and tell him you need to talk to him." I said, "Okay."

From my office phone, I buzzed his office and told him I needed to talk with him. He was busy but told me he would call me back and see me as soon as he was free. I said, "Okay."

In a very short time, he called back and invited me into his office. I entered and took a seat while he finished a couple more phone conversations. Once done, he looked at me and said, "What do you want?" I tried but I couldn't open my mouth. Then he said, "You're not leaving, are you?" I still couldn't say a word, so I nodded my head to affirm that I was leaving. Then he said, "Not today I hope." Again, I couldn't say a word, so I nodded my head to say yes. His response was so positive, it was almost unbelievable. He told me that I could come back anytime I wanted to work at the radio station. "What will you be doing?" he asked. I shared with him that I was starting my own magazine. He wished me success and I walked out.

God had shut my mouth and let the radio station owner tell me what I wanted to tell him. Therefore, quitting my job without any prior notice ended on a positive note instead of a negative one. I was amazed but a bit scared as I drove home after quitting my job to start my own business. But you have to know that you can do it if God told you to do it.

The road ahead was difficult but fulfilling and rewarding. Operating a magazine is a tough business but I had the DNA for the task. I was driven, relentless, and able to wear many hats gracefully under pressure. The magazine afforded me the opportunity to meet and interview a diversity of people, locally, nationally, and internationally:

Mrs. Coretta Scott King and Yolanda King, Zig Ziglar, Attorney Johnny Cochran, Florence Griffin Joyner, Ambassador Andrew Young, General Colin Powell, Rev. Jesse Jackson, Bishop T.D. Jakes, Dr. Myles Munroe, CeCe Winans, Sugar Ray Leonard, and many others. I learned to lead and manage a staff of writers, graphic designers, photographers, artists, and salespersons, and to develop business relationships with decision-makers in corporations that purchased advertising in the magazine. I had to know my worth as I sat at the table in meetings, facing a room full of business men. Amazingly, God had prepared me and was with me.

The call to ministry in 1989 brought me face to face with sexism in the church. The Baptist denomination that I had been a part of all my life did not ordain women. I had been a member at that church since I first came to Ohio at age 13 because my mom's membership there. I had only seen male pastors and ministers all my life. Although women were Sunday school teachers, missionaries, choir directors, singers, and placed over various auxiliaries, none were allowed in the pulpit. Until I was called into ministry, it wasn't a problem.

After God spoke to me three times, telling me He wanted me to preach the gospel, it was perfectly clear. I had a meeting with my pastor to give him the news, knowing his stance on women ministers. He did not ordain women, period. I told him I knew his position on ordaining women, but I had to tell him about God's call on my life. Following the meeting, I felt better because it was off my chest. It was painful to watch man after man become ordained into ministry. I was frustrated and tried to leave several times. I asked, "Father God, what do you want me to do?" He replied, "Continue teaching the children in Sunday school because it's important to me."

Being busy running the magazine helped me endure the disappointment. I was so busy I didn't have time to worry about church politics. As time went on, I was called to speak and preach because I became known nationally through *Purpose* Magazine. I remained at that church for ten additional years. When God released me, he sent me to Nassau, Bahamas, where the late Dr. Myles Munroe ordained me for international ministry. Two years later, in 2001, I was ordained locally by Apostles Eric and Carolyn Warren at their nondenominational ministry, Equippers City Church. It was a long wait, but I received double blessings.

When suffering from sexism, racism, or any other ism, it is important to understand who you are. Remember, don't take it personally. It is not your spiritual defect unless you make it yours; it's theirs.

There are many challenges and trials in life. In 2008, after living in the Washington, D.C. area, I encountered double trouble. I lost advertising during the economic crisis during President George Bush's term and when President Barack Obama began his first term. I incurred significant debt trying to keep the magazine going. Life was further complicated when I discovered that my mother was diagnosed with dementia. It was a trying time, to say the least. I went from CEO to caregiver and had to trust God because there was no other way to get through the trial. Although painful, I had to understand with my whole spirit, soul, and body, that I was alright and still Ella, even when I couldn't publish a printed magazine and do all the things I was used to doing. I let go of many of my ambitions to take care of Mom for eleven years, until her recent death in March of 2019. God gave me strength and grace to care for her and I'm a better person because of it. My love for Mom is so strong, and I did my best to insure her comfort and dignity. Through my experience of serving Mom, I discovered a part of me that I did not know existed—a part of my genuine worth as servant of God, a daughter, and a minister.

As finish this chapter, I'm beginning a new chapter in my life. And, as I grieve the death of my mother, I rejoice in the Spirit for the refreshed vision God has given me to fulfill in this season.

About the Author

Ella Coleman is an inspirational speaker, author, vision consultant, president of Ellavation Publishing, and publisher of *Purpose Magazine*. Please visit her websites at www.EllaColeman.net or www.PurposeMagazine.com or contact her at Ella@EllaColeman.net.

Dr. Evelyn Bethune

To Truly Know and Love God is to be Infused with His Strength

Every day I wake up knowing that I am developing my understanding of what my worth is as a woman. It was not always that way. For most of my adult life, I have focused on helping others recognize their worth, while taking for granted that I too had value. I was basing my measure of self-worth on how others saw me. It was also attached to being measured by the knowledge that I am the granddaughter of Dr. Mary McLeod Bethune. With that relationship comes an enormous responsibility, real and imagined, of standards that MUST be met. My grandmother is an internationally acclaimed icon and though she died in 1955, her legacy and the seeds she planted are still producing fruit.

She was GREAT and growing up in the shadow of her greatness was what one of my brothers described as both a blessing and a curse. The curse comes from the preconceived notions that people have once they know our relationship. The blessing is the DNA that God saw fit to attach to us. Navigating those waters can be rewarding, even in the difficulty. For most of my life, my worth has been measured by how well I measured up to the legacy that was left to us.

I do not strive for greatness because of who Mary Jane McLeod Bethune is to the world. I have always desired to achieve because of who she is to my family. Her blood is my blood, and that strength within her also flows in me. I excel because it is in my nature to do so, it is a part of my cultural DNA. Even with that said, there have been times that I have faltered, I have stumbled, and I have sometimes fallen on my face, but I always knew to call on the name of Jesus. I can never remember a time that I did not believe in God; even when I did not believe in myself. There was always something in my spirit that kept me close to God.

For a very long time, like Peter, I tried to deny the legacy that my grandmother left us, mistakenly thinking that it resided in the material trappings of buildings or currency. I felt that because our family was systematically separated from the visual legacy that carried our name, we were also separated from all that connected us to our ancestors. But GOD has a way of making it plain.

Then the Lord answered me and said:

Write the vision and make it plain on tablets,
that he may run who reads it.

For the vision is yet for an appointed time;

But at the end it will speak, and it will not lie.

Though it tarries, wait for it; because it will

surely come, it will not tarry. (Habakkuk 2:2,3)

In the book of Habakkuk, God instructs His people to not only talk about and meditate on their dreams and inspirations, but to also write them down. Seeing the words helps to remind you of your destiny and makes it more real to you and anyone who reads it. It is important to keep focused during those months or years of preparation. There is a time and season for everything; however long it may seem, your time is coming. Continuing to observe the vision builds unity within the people.

My mother used to tell me that I was born to write. I was writing at a very early age and as a very young person, (elementary school) I wrote notes to her and my dad when they would take a position on something that differed from what I thought they should. I would write to them and explain why I thought they should do something different. Too funny. I love the art of writing because it allows the writer to express their thoughts, uninterrupted. Writing is a method of healing as well.

It opens wounds so that a healing salve can be applied. It allows for introspection of past deeds as well as providing a mechanism to work through the details of plans for the future. You see, in our heads, deeds of the past are done and pushed into our closed files, yet still leaving the residue of consequences. Plans for the future are always complete in our minds but without the details needed for successful completion. Sometimes, because we do not revisit deeds of the past, those completed plans get side tracked or derailed because of not dealing with the mistakes of past endeavors. Writing it down, making it plain, allows us to take an honest look, deal with our mistakes, heal and move forward. Write the vision, make it plain...

At 66 years of age, I have FINALLY come to know my worth. Not my worth as the granddaughter, the daughter, the wife, the mother, the sister, the friend, the advisor, or any external title, but as Evelyn. My worth as a woman was hidden behind so many walls because we live in a world prone to discount women collectively, and Black women in particular. Some of those walls/obstacles, I controlled but most were determined by society and accepted as the "standard". For the most part, I felt I didn't measure up. No matter how smart, how accomplished or sought after I was, I never thought it was for me. I did not know my worth. I felt I was not worthy and because I felt that way, I was also willing to accept less than I deserved. I learned very early how to hide my true feelings in business as well as personal relationships. Even as a child, I clearly understood that because of who we were, there were certain things, behaviors, that were expected. In my relationships, I would not ask the hard questions because I was afraid of the answer. I did not want to be rejected. But rejection is a part of living so no matter what I did, rejection would come, and I would add another layer to the mask.

For over fifty years, I have smothered my responses, my true feelings, many of my thoughts and ideas, and worked diligently to heal the wounded, and bolster the egos of those around me, especially the men of my relationships and marriages. What usually happens is I will acquiesce until I can't take it anymore and then the boil comes to a head and pops. That is what happens when I allow myself to be relegated to a position that makes me feel less than. The frustration is internalized and shows itself in various ways; usually it is not positive. It can be physical illness and most especially depression which can be life threatening. In this life's journey, I have had times of self-doubt so deep that I would have taken my own life had it not been for the depth of love I have for my family. I could not do that to them and leave them wondering if it was because of something they did or did not do. I am grateful to God for giving me the family I have, especially my children and my grandson. I see the love of God through them daily.

God is doing a mighty work in me. The past four years have been very hard on our family. We are very close and though miles separate us in some cases, we are in contact daily. On Easter Sunday 2015, my nephew Jarvis died of a massive heart attack at the age of 34, just as he was beginning a new business, with a beautiful wife and two incredible children. He was a bright and shining star, whose faith in God was evident in the way he lived his life and the beauty of how he lifted others. Just as we thought we might feel the pain a bit less, our brother, Hobson, died of injuries he sustained when he was hit head on while riding his motorcycle. July 2017. The depth of my sadness still overtakes me, and I am still trying to press my way through. In my quest to be strong for others, I have not allowed anyone to be strong for me. I wear the mask. I have kept my relationship with God but not at the level that I should nor the level that He desires. I have heard His voice say, "slow down," pay attention," and "keep my commandments." I was not obedient. I was fully engaged in too many things that distracted me from the purpose God placed in me and found it easy to take short cuts because I was not staying close to Him. I thought that if I could stay so busy that I could not think, the hurt would lesson. It didn't. Because I didn't know my worth, I didn't feel I was worthy of a deep relationship with God, though I desired that relationship. I would not get still and focus on developing it because I did not want to be rejected by God. On the surface, I knew Jesus died to make sure I would not be rejected. I have said the words a million times but to others, not internalizing them for myself. I trust God. I just didn't trust myself.

The year 2017 was also the year I began to make a series of mistakes in judgement and decision-making that would demand a change in my focus. I broke a trust relationship, never intending to do so but as the saying goes, "the road to hell is paved with good intentions." Because of my mistake in judgement, I hurt people that I care for deeply and placed my family in a very embarrassing position. People that I thought were close friends, stepped away from me and the haters, who don't like me anyway, enjoyed the drama. It all came to a head in April of 2018. You see, I could not clean up the mess I made fast enough, though I was trying. Sometimes, in order to get our attention, God allows us to hit our heads on the concrete. We must get bloody before we get still and quiet, bow our heads and listen to what He has to say. Fear causes foolish actions. There is no fear in God. In the midst of a horrible situation that may require me to lose my freedom for a moment, God is doing a mighty work in me. "They can lock me up, but they can't lock God out." That is true whether you are in physical jail or mental jail. God is always there; we have but to call on the name of Jesus. If nothing else is gained from the experiences that I am sharing I hope one thing is clear: we must never give up on ourselves. Many times, the way will not be clear, and we may not be sure of what to do. The clarity will come as you get closer to your spiritual self and open your mind, body and soul to the Word of God.

I can feel a mighty work of God and I see Him moving obstacles out of my path. I feel His presence and I hear His instruction. What was once a feeling of defeat has been replaced with a sense of very defined purpose. God has said to me that no matter what the decision is, He will give me what I need to get to the other side of it. Circumstance has slowed me down and cleared some people out of my life that were only in my life because of what they thought I could do for them. Too much of my time has been spent building for others what God meant for me to build for Him.

Throughout my life I have experienced what I now call "fleeting moments of insanity." These moments have put distance between me and God and the work He designed for me. These moments are anchored in fear, and not knowing my own worth as a woman. I just wrote a piece for a guest blog that explains what this means:

"We all have them... moments when we felt that we were losing our minds. Moments when we found ourselves in situations that hold us hostage, wondering how we got there; yet knowing it was of our own making, but still feeling as if we had been forced into it. Fleeting moments of insanity. These are the moments when we wish we could roll back the hands of time and do something different, but we can't. We regret our actions, our hasty response, our crazy decision, our really wrong choices but it is too late to take it back. Now what? Own it. Take responsibility for it and prepare to deal with the consequences. Oh yes... there will be consequences.

Depending on how major or minor the mess is that you have created, the consequences may be manageable or take away your freedom. The one thing that you can count on is that the penalty for your actions will always be more than you want to pay. You may lose friends, your reputation may take a temporary hit or be ruined forever, your finances may suffer, and your employability may become questionable. You may also cause harm to those you love and lose the respect of those that matter to you. More than likely the action that brought you to this point was filled with good intentions but never shared with those you needed to include in the decision.

*TRUST ISSUES can cost you everything. Trust God. Not knowing your own value can lead to you make irrational decisions that leave you wondering what exactly you were thinking. God created you intentionally, not by accident, therefore, you have great value. FEAR leads to desperation and desperation to acts of insanity, fleeting moments of insanity that can leave lasting effects. **There is NO FEAR in God.**"*

When I decide and I leave God out of the equation, it will always be a bad choice. In the past few months, God has shown me that His love for me is unconditional and no matter what the issue is, He will always be there. He will also send tangible signs so I don't have to try to figure it out. I just simply must know that He is offering me the same sustenance that I tell others He has for them.

This project is one of those tangible signs that better days are coming. My family and the incredible circle of strong, praying, friends who encourage me daily are another sign. I had to have a valley experience to understand my true worth. I am strong, I am determined, I am beautifully and wonderfully made. God has placed creativity in me, and it is time to let my little light shine based on my own value.

Yes, I am the granddaughter of Mary, daughter of Albert and Elizabeth, sister, mother, grandmother, friend, etc., but first and foremost, I am Evelyn, Woman of God...Beautiful, Beloved, Priceless!

About the Author

Dr. Evelyn Bethune, selected as A Phenomenal Woman 2015 and one of the Most Influential Women in Business for 2012 and 2014 by the *Daytona Beach Business Journal*, is the granddaughter of Dr. Mary McLeod Bethune and CEO of The Bethune Group MMB, Inc. (TBG, Inc.). As a part of TBG, Inc., she founded MMB Institute, a mentoring and instructional foundation for people of all ages but, in particular, young people. She is an Amazon best-selling author, lecturer, radio program host, and motivational speaker. One of the goals of Dr. Evelyn Bethune is to continue the work of expanding knowledge of Dr. Mary Mcleod Bethune, ensuring growth and development of her legacy by encouraging and promoting education and community service on a variety of platforms.

Over the years, Dr. Evelyn Bethune has mentored hundreds of students through high school, college and beyond. She has a passion for helping solve problems and bringing a positive end to what can sometimes be difficult situations. Dr. Bethune instructs "non-violent" communications, oral and physical (body language) and promotes an environment of consensus. She is at her best when she is serving the public.

She may be contacted by email at docbethune@tbginc.org or by writing to Dr. Evelyn Bethune, The Bethune Group, MMB, Inc., P.O. Box 2008, Daytona Beach, FL 32115, (386) 301-5762.

Fallon Archer

The Council

Nervously I stood in the doorway next to the deserted circular drive, biting the side of my thumb and leaning on the side of my shoe. I heard my mother's voice over my right shoulder, "Stop, before you ruin the shoes." My cousin, Sharron, was just as stern in her tone, and she was equally as hard to ignore. "Don't bite your thumb, Hootchie." Hearing her call me by my nickname from infancy felt weird in the present circumstance. I stopped biting and looked for what seemed to be the 400th time, pass the parking lot and onto the street. As always, my best friend of fourteen years was late.

Audibly I sighed as I shifted my weight onto my other foot. *Where the heck was Brandy?* Like a response to my impatience, a shiny black sprinter van slowed and turned off the main street before coming to a stop in front of me. The driver, a middle-aged black man, had close cut salt and pepper hair and sad eyes. His shirt and his slacks were crisp. Both black.

He said a somber hello and nodded in my direction before beginning to open the rear doors for Brandy. He stopped and at looked at me before the second door was opened. I had been waiting over an hour standing rigidly in my heels and new dress. I wanted him to hurry. Time was running short and there was much to do.

"Excuse me, sir, what are we waiting for?"

"I have to wait for someone to help me with…" his voice trailed off respectfully.

"Oh, no… we don't have to wait I can help," I said matter-of-factly.

A second of silence and then he laughed, "Oh no… you can't do that."

I'm sure the sight of me standing there in my lacy dress and high heels wasn't exactly looking like I was ready or even able to do any manual labor.

"You can't…" the driver repeated, looking incredulously as I placed my handbag on the retaining wall and rejoined him.

His sad eyes were wide now, and he opened his mouth as if to say more but the look on my face stopped him. For me, this was neither a discussion nor a debate. A defeated man, he threw up his weathered hands in a gesture of mock submission, opened the doors completely, then excused himself to disappear through the doors I had just come through. I stepped up to the opening of the van and looked inside.

As I reached out one hand, I touched the casket holding my best friend and confidant in the whole world. The cold wood felt like stone under my hand. It was real. This whole week I spent fighting the reality of losing her. The wraith of grief that screamed and pried at the edges of my sanity was real. It was all real. As real as the sun that put shadows at my feet or the feel of the air conditioning in the van that made goosepimples along my exposed forearm. *Don't cry you can't cry.*

The driver returned pushing what looked like a very tall coffee table with wheels. He looked around, hopeful, as if he were praying that someone would stop me last minute. No such luck. There wasn't anyone else around except the elderly woman behind the desk inside. I looked back toward the rear of the property for any other cars. None. It was just the driver and I… and my silent friend, forever quiet. *Stop, don't cry.*

When he was at last convinced that no savior was coming, he relented, and we locked the wheels of the dolly/table in place.

At his instruction I put one hand on the ornate golden handle of her casket, one heeled foot on the bumper and pulled. I thought I heard him say that I should be careful and that she was heavy, but I was more concerned with the weight of what I had to do and the importance of such a task for her entire family. Many of whom stood with me in the hospital, hurt, angry and shocked the day the unthinkable happened.

That day was like a nightmare I couldn't wake up from, couldn't forget.

As I walked into my apartment building, my phone started notifying me of a call on Facebook Messenger. Instinctively I reached for the phone and was surprised to see Brandy's husband's face pictured above the ringing phone icon. Why is she calling me from his phone, I thought? Maybe she lost hers or it was dead.

"Hello?"

"HELLO?!!!!!"

The tears in his voice made it shaky and hard to understand. My first thought was Nana and Papa, her elderly parents. Something must have happened.

"Brandy's in the hospital." My heart dropped, and I moved into action.

I don't remember the thirteen-minute drive, moving on auto pilot, taking the same trip that I had taken many times over to pick her up from her job at the very same hospital.

Memories of our rushed lunches, when she only had thirty minutes to spare and half of that time we spent in hysterics. We would find any place close to the hospital to eat because she had patients to get back to.

"You got it?'

The sudden closeness of the van driver's voice startled me. When had he moved to my left side?

My voice cracked as I answered him.

"Yes, I think so."

He checked to make sure she was settled securely on the coffee table chariot and moved her to a small dimly lit room with an altar and empty pews. He opened the casket, removed a lace cloth from her face and left us alone. I stood with my hands on the side of the coffer and stared down at her. She appeared asleep but for the stillness of her. There was no smile playing on her lips, no life in her cheeks. She wasn't herself and yet she was.

I stood there, wanting to cry and searching for some meaningful words. In the end, I just spoke to her like I always had, like an annoying little sister.

"Your last appointment ON EARTH and you couldn't be on time? Just HAD to be late."

I smiled despite the awkwardness of the moment. My mother and my cousin laughed. They both knew how silly and close she and I were. Their quiet laughter reminded me of the hours Brandy and I spent talking. About our goals, our crushes, her children, our divorces.

Then I cried.

I wept for all the things she had planned to do and the milestones in my life she would miss. I cried in pain for the sudden way she was taken away. I ached for her four children and her granddaughter who never got the chance to say goodbye, because they never thought they would have to. Not now. Never this soon. She was only thirty-nine years old. I shook with anger thinking of all the time she should have had left. SHE WAS SUPPOSED TO HAVE MORE TIME!

"That's enough Hooch, you're ok." Even quietly my cousin's voice seemed to ring out in the still silence of the room. She was right that was enough. Okay focus up. Time to work.

I wiped my face and began the task of doing her hair and makeup. Eerily enough the day before she died, she had gotten full spa services: eye brows waxed, eye lash extensions and a beautiful purple manicure. Even in death she was stunning.

First to style her hair in the side part she always wore, then her makeup and her glasses (it wasn't right without them.) And finally, her signature red lips.

"She looks good baby." I turned for one last look at my friend. My sister. My heart. I spoke aloud to my mother and cousin as if they were still living, "yea, she does."

I left that funeral home forever changed.

Six months prior, I lost my closest first cousin, Sharron, to a rare heart disease. She fought and outlived her diagnosis by years, succumbing after seven years of treatments, oxygen and medication changes. While I was glad she was at rest and no longer in pain, I was devastated. Sharron raised me.

She taught me AP trigonometry when the class work went well beyond my parents' level of skill. Over the years, she fixed any object that I was SURE was broken forever (including my heart a few times).

She was a phenomenal woman who knew the significance of anything and rested in how you could use it to help others. She knew the value of a kind word, a care package. She was the person in the family who always had a genuine ear for our rambling kid conversations. She understood that the importance wasn't in the nonsense message we were conveying but in cultivating an environment where children feel comfortable expressing themselves. You could talk to her about anything.

That carried over seamlessly into adulthood. Buying a used car? Take Sharron with you, she knows what to check. Relocating? She knew the best areas for your budget and how to get anything you needed once moving day arrived. She was a fixer. And my main go- to for my ever-present teen complaints. About what? My mother of course!

Vanessa. Born in the mid-1950s during a time of social propriety and manners, she was a stickler for etiquette and intense to grow up under. She lived for decorum and knew hundreds of fashion rules. She also worked corporately most of her life, so she knew the secret. She knew that when working in environments full of men who look nothing like you, nor are as qualified, your success and survival depend on being sharp, thick-skinned, and fearless.

Those lessons I learned vicariously as I watched her over the years. I witnessed her mastery of cake design before there were cake challenges and online tutorials. She mastered sewing, event planning, gemology, pharmacology and anything else she set her mind to doing. She was dynamic. Didn't cut corners and never let me. I was never to give less than a full effort, never to embarrass myself or my family. I learned to walk gracefully in heels as high as three inches before second grade. To stoop with knees bent to the side and never ever to bend at the waist when in a dress.

She was a champion for me in the public school system., challenging them when my teachers told her I was too young to be reading the sex and violence in the Jackie Collins and Alice Walker books my aunt shared with me. She didn't waiver where I was concerned. By the time I hit fourth grade, I was not only in challenge classes, reading at a 12th grade level, but I was doing it in bowties, pencil skirts, and heels.

She taught me that grace and strength aren't mutually exclusive, that's a woman's worth is not variant; more than an ideal to glorify, it was immutable.

It wasn't based on the length of her skirt, her socio-economic standing, nor her ability to get or keep a man. It's in the way she treats others, the way she allows others to treat her and in the undeniable effort she puts into her work and her family. A woman's merit is binding, absolute and worth fighting for.

Cancer took my mother in 2006. Before that, she did so much for countless others. She was befriended and beloved by so many that thirteen years later, I am still running into people asking about 'Nessa.

Sharron and Vanessa taught me invaluable lessons. And they were both gone. If having Brandy to go to in my mourning was the only thing that kept me going, I was going to have to accept the reality that whether I choose to fall or fly, sink or soar, I would be doing it alone.

I wasn't sure what that looked like. I couldn't imagine what I would be without her.

The keys clutched tightly in my fist started a dull ache in the center of my palm, much like a beacon rousing me from my own thoughts. There were a few cars in the lot now, I hadn't even noticed their arrival. *How long have I been standing here?* I opened the door to my rental car and slid into the seat. Up until this point, I was operating in a somewhat anaesthetized state. Now, the weight of what I had just done for my friend seemed to descend onto me. My shoulders stooped and I fell apart. The memories I had been trying to stave off all afternoon came flooding in.

Brandy, round and pregnant waving at me from the curb as I drove away in a U-Haul bound for a new life on the other side of the country.

Brandy in her wedding dress wiping tears as she walked with her dad down the aisle.

Brandy couponing like a pro and giving the goods away to one or more church or youth groups.

The way she threw her head back and the wheezing sound she made when she laughed was TOO funny.

The silly voices she assigned to the dolls in her house, who would either catcall you or verbally assault you, and you never knew which one it would be.

She was a woman who lived and livened every room she entered. A woman who nursed professionally because it was just who she was.

She was a rock of unwavering faith for her family, and for me as well. She saw me through the death of my mother and cousin, both of whom absolutely loved her.

On nights when I wasn't sure that I would see the sun come up, she reassured me. On days when I didn't eat and didn't care, she did. Brandy listened without tiring or judging and always understood my grief over losing them. And now she was with them, somewhere I couldn't go.

Today, I simply call them, "The Council." A spiritual assembly of all the best parts of myself. I take the hard choices, the bad times, even my good news to them and I feel comforted knowing each of them has guided me in a unique way.

My mother keeps my head tilted high when I walk. Her words ring true decades later and resound in my heart. She is the grace in my step, the respect I command, and the articulation with which I speak.

My cousin reminds me that everything broken is not yet lost. She is the glue I use to mend the sometimes-shattered parts of my life. A reason to always try and try again.

My friend holds my hand when I don't feel strong enough. A constant source of trust and strength, she is the light of genuine love by which I care for others. She is the smile on my lips and the laughter that comes from my soul.

My Council. Three very capable ladies whose wealth of life experiences I use to tap into my own worth.

Our lives are far from perfect. There are set backs and failures and we must learn those things are NOT the quantifier by which we gauge our value, our worth, as women. It is our unflinching ability to get back up, with elegance, and keep not only our faith, but our crown, intact… that's what truly matters.

About the Author

Fallon Archer is a native of Chicago, Illinois. She can be reached via email at Archer4205@gmail.com.

Jai A. Darden

Loving a Woman of Worth

"Always make her feel special, never go to bed angry, talk it out – never leave things unsettled, do the small things for her – they matter, and tell her that you love her – she should hear it often from you."
~Clara D. Darden (Mom)

I can remember it as if it were yesterday. It would be the last time my mom would visit my home. My wife and I gave my oldest son a birthday party to remember. He was turning the Big "3," and we went all out to say the least. He was our only child at the time, and we were excited young parents.

Present were friends from his preschool, young cousins, grandparents, aunts, uncles, and some of our closest friends. The kids played games, did face painting, played outside on an inflatable Spiderman jumping house, and hoped for tons of candy from the piñata that they took turns hitting.

I was overjoyed it was turning out to be a marvelous day. My son was having the time of his life, and all the invited guests were enjoying themselves. My wife and I were elated to have all the people we cared deeply about in the same house. It wasn't often that we were able to gather everyone together this way. This was truly a special day.

I walked around the house making sure everyone was having a good time. Now at this time, it was late into the party and some people had begun to leave. As I left the kitchen to enter the family room where everyone was, I caught my mom out the corner of my eye. She was standing, using her walker, down the hall at the front of the house where the entrance of the formal dining room was.

I wondered to whom she was speaking. I could not see anyone else from where I was positioned. One thing was for sure, she was captivated by something in that room. I began to walk slowly in her direction, not wanting to startle her or interrupt a discussion.

As I approached the entrance, my mom was there speaking with one of my wife's friends. They were wrapping up their talk as I entered the room. Of course, I told them to continue and I would leave, but they insisted that they had completed their visit and my wife's friend left.

I stood there looking at my mom as she stared at the dining table. She glanced upward to view the painting that hung on the wall; then she looked over to the window treatment. I could tell she was admiring the room and everything about it. She asked me if I had painted the room, and I was pleased to tell her that I had. It was the first room that I had painted after moving into the house.

She smiled at me with the most heart-warming smile I had ever seen. Then she tilted her head, stood erect and said to me, *"Always make her feel special, never go to bed angry, talk it out – never leave things unsettled, do the small things for her – they matter, and tell her that you love her – she should hear it often from you."*

I was a little confused because this statement came from out of nowhere. I asked her what she meant, why she had given this advice, and why now? At first, she gave no reaction or response. She simply looked back over the room as to gather her thoughts. I stood there wondering what was racing through my mom's mind.

You see, she was intuitive, present in the moment, and always centered. She was a praying woman who got up every morning at 3:00 to seek guidance from God. She was in tune with the world around her and read often to raise her level of consciousness. My mom was a woman of courage. She had been sick for many years and had some close calls, almost losing her battle on several occasions. By the grace of God, she was still standing. She never complained or questioned why; she just kept pushing with a beautiful smile that could melt hearts and always found an encouraging word to offer. As she stood there, I could tell that she was searching for the words to express what she had on her heart to say to me.

Then suddenly, the silence was broken.

My mom began to tell me how lovely the room was and how she could tell that there was a lot of thought, time, and effort put into making this room a special place.

Then she asked, "Have you ever had dinner in this room?"

"No ma'am", I replied.

"How long have you been living here?"

"About eighteen months now."

Then she asked, "Why haven't you used it? What are you waiting on?"

I stood there first trying to understand the reasoning for all the questions. Secondly, I did not have a good answer. "I don't know Mom. I guess I am waiting on a good time to do it."

With a tender smile she continued, "Didn't you paint and decorate this room? It looks nice. You did a great job, and everything is in its place. Why did you do it? Why did you spend the time doing all of this?"

I thought for a moment and responded, "I figured this would be a place to make special memories, memories we could cherish for the rest of our lives. We could have special dinners with the family, possibly host Thanksgiving here one year. This room represents times for special moments, Mom."

Then she spoke words that will live with me forever, "Just as you spent your valuable time making this room beautiful so that memories could be created, you need to make sure your wife feels that you are putting in the effort to create special memories with her. Make her feel special; make her feel appreciated and needed. Talk with each other; share your goals and dreams and work to reach them together. Be an unbreakable team. You will not always agree but let nothing stand between you and her. Before your head falls on your pillow, fix it and get it right. Forgive because tomorrow is not promised.

Remember the little things. You do not have to spend much money or any at all to make a big impact. Remembering dates, times, and moments that mean so much to her will make her feel like you care. Be present, make time for her, and don't be distracted.

Don't assume she knows you love her; tell her you love her. And do it often."

I stood there in awe as I listened. I was encapsulated by her words of wisdom.

Just I thought she was finished, she concluded with these words, "Have a dinner in this room just for you and her. She will appreciate it and remember it for the rest of her life. But don't stop there. Keep making memories like that no matter where you live. Do that for me."

I answered with tears in my eyes, "Yes Momma. I will do it. I promise."

She nodded her head, smiled, and began to leave the room.

We returned to the family room where everyone else was assembled. A few moments after entering the room, she told my dad that she was ready to go home. I escorted my parents out to the car, gave them a hug, and wished them traveling grace because they lived approximately one hundred miles from me at the time.

After everyone had gone home, I went back to the dining room and replayed what my mom had shared with me. I stood there quietly, rehashing every word. My wife walked into the room and asked me what I was doing. I simply told her that I was admiring the room. For months, I would hold close the words that my mom shared with me that evening.

Only months later, my beloved mom would go to be with The Lord. Her passing took a toll on me; she was truly a favored and blessed woman filled with love and wisdom. I asked God to grant me peace and the strength to live up to the expectations my mom had for me. I made it a point to follow through on the things that she shared with me that faithful night.

Things were becoming clearer. My mom had placed a challenge on me. She had challenged me to be the 'Next Level" man she knew I could become. She would often tell me that she had fought for so long to live and not die so she could see her baby boy grow up and walk into his purpose and achieve some of his dreams. Well, she had been blessed to see me achieve much in the world of academics, business, and within my community. I had a family now, and we were doing well. However, she recognized that for me to truly reach the pinnacles of success, I would have to know my wife's worth and honor her in that sense as we walked the journey of life together.

Mom needed me to fully comprehend and get into my spirit Proverbs 18:22, "He who finds a wife finds what is good and receives favor from the LORD." I was blessed to find a wife and not just a woman. Yes, I could have accomplished what I had up to that point alone and unmarried, but it would not have happened as quickly, as profoundly, and it would not have been as sweet. I found favor. I was blessed. And my mom wanted me to know it.

She needed me to understand the value of what I was blessed to have, a Proverbs 31:10 wife. "An excellent woman [one who is spiritual, capable, intelligent, and virtuous], who is he who can find her? Her value is more precious than jewels *and* her worth is far above rubies *or* pearls." AMP

She was telling me to take care of home. How I treated my wife would spill over in all other areas of my life. Adhering to this principle, I made sure I did not go to bed upset or angry. I remembered the little things and made sure I was present. A day did not go by without me saying the words, I love you.

One thing was for sure, that dining room was filled with memories. I would often go into that room and stand in the very place my mom and I had had that incredible conversation. I would close my eyes and hear her voice speaking those life-changing words to me. There was one problem; I had not yet had dinner in the dining room. I had made a promise. It had to be fulfilled.

The next major holiday was Thanksgiving. I asked my dad if he would be okay if we hosted Thanksgiving at our home. He quickly agreed, and it was so fulfilling to have the family over to enjoy this holiday. What made it even more gratifying was I had followed through on having dinner there. Still, I had not done all mom had asked. She wanted me to have a special dinner with and for my wife in that room.

It was important to me to ensure that the time I selected for our dinner was special. As I waited for the perfect time, time quickly moved on and the perfect time never came. A few years later, we would place our home on the market for sell. We were blessed to receive several offers quickly; we accepted an offer within four days of the house being placed on the market. Now I had to do it and do it now.

I alerted my wife that I would be taking her to a celebration dinner. I asked her to take out her favorite going-out-on-the-town dress and shoes. Her response was priceless; she was filled with excitement. Everyday leading up to the special evening she would ask for details such as the name of the restaurant, the type of atmosphere, and the type of food.

The day had arrived, and I can still remember how my heart raced in anticipation. I wanted so much for the evening to go off without a hitch. As the time drew near, I asked her to get dressed and not come out of the room until I came to get her. This created even more suspense for her.

While she was in the room getting dressed, I transformed the dining room with candles and soft music. The room was imbued with an array of colorful flowers. One would have thought that the dining room was part of an exclusive five-star restaurant. The ambiance had to be just right for this momentous occasion. The five-course meal we would eat that evening was catered by one of her favorite restaurants.

Once everything was in its place, I went into our room where she was sitting patiently. What I saw stopped me in my tracks; she was breathtaking. Her hair was beautifully done, her make-up was spectacular, and the dress she was wearing appeared to have been made specifically for her.

I took a quick shower and put on my black suit. I was ready to take my wife to dinner. I asked, "Are you ready to go?" She said, "Yes, I'm hungry."

I held out my arm as to escort her and said, "Let's go to dinner." I walked her slowly down the hall to the front of the house toward the dining room. I could see her looking at me somewhat confused, but I kept my eyes straight ahead. As I walked, I could hear my mom's voice telling me to make my wife feel that she was worth all of this and more.

We took our seats at the table, and I watched as she glanced around taking everything in. I explained I would be both her server and date for the evening. We enjoyed the food and the music as it played softly in the background. We talked about everything; there were no boundaries. We discussed our goals and dreams for ourselves personally, together, and for our family. We laughed as we reminisced about old funny times we had experienced in the past. Time as we knew it had paused just for us. This time together was majestic. I asked her to dance, and she eagerly obliged.

While we danced, my wife looked into my eyes and whispered, "You told me that this was a celebration dinner, but you didn't tell me what we are celebrating." I looked back into her eyes as she anticipated my response. I simply replied, "You."

Words cannot describe the look she gave me. She hugged me tight as to say I will never let you go. She thanked and told me that that evening had been one, of if not the best, of her life.

At the time of writing this some ten plus years later, I asked my wife if she could remember that evening's dinner. She did. To my amazement, she recalled specific details I had forgotten, intricate details that stood out to her. She described in detail the degree of lighting in the room and even the food we ate. She smiled and said, "Yes, I remember it. It was nice."

Mom was right; it was a moment in time my wife would never forget.

About the Author

Jai A. Darden helps businesses produce sustainable revenue and increased profits by building lifelong relationships with their customers and clients. He is a trusted advisor to many CEOs and executives and frequents the boardrooms of some of the most successful and influential companies in the country. Subject matter experts, authors, and solopreneurs seek out Jai's guidance in producing systems to generate income based on their knowledge, experience, and skill.

If you would like to learn more about Jai and how he may be able to help you grow your business, connect with him at www.jaidarden.com or call (888) 391-1008. Authors, subject matter experts, or solopreneurs looking to generate more business and revenue go to: www.jaidarden.com/talk.

Jamela Johnson

The Broken Are More Evolved

Have you ever questioned your own self-worth and/or felt as if your past circumstances have held you back?... are holding you back? Let me assure you that if you said yes to this question, you must no longer allow your past to keep you locked in like a prisoner. The key word here is "allow." You see, YOU have the power within you to serve an eviction notice to every single one of your unfortunate circumstances that have made a home in your mind like a pack of squatters.

At some point in your life you may have found yourself taking a step back and examining where you are and wondering "how on earth did I get here?' or "I didn't plan for things to be like this, what happened?" You see, most of us, if we're honest with ourselves, have been traveling a path led by our unfortunate circumstances. Our paths can typically be traced back to our childhood and things that occurred during those times. For me it wasn't any different, except I tried to bury those things as if they had no effect on me. I remember being this shy and quiet girl unable to confidently speak to strangers or even family members for that matter. My trust in people had been shattered by various relationships from childhood well into adulthood.

As a girl, I figured this was just who I was. I was born this way. At the time, I didn't know I had a fear of and mistrust for people because of the things that had been done to me nor did I acknowledge those things. You see, from my first moments of recollection, I had been repeatedly molested by people I should have been able to trust. You wouldn't expect to be hurt by family or close friends of the family, right?

On the outside I appeared to continue the natural development of children, exploring and growing. I would even say I was very daring. One might even say I was fierce! I can remember climbing the roof of our house when I was four years old, running in and out of old abandoned homes playing a game of hide and seek, and stealing money out of my mamma's coin jar (regularly). I even took a chug of her cognac that sat on the side of her bed. (That stuff liked to have ripped my throat and chest right out of body, might I add.) Through all of that, I was still this little girl who didn't feel worthy and I later became a woman who didn't feel worthy. I withdrew from anything that put too much focus on me, that put me out front to be looked at by others.

I'll never forget the incident in junior high during my first track meet. I'd like to think I was pretty fast, but no one will ever know just how fast, because I chose to sabotage my own results. Imagine, gearing up to run the 200-meter race, excited because you knew your potential. However, coming out of the curve, you notice you're neck and neck with the star runner. In your mind you're excited because you know you haven't even tapped into your full potential, but your thoughts begin to tell you that you're not supposed to beat her! And just like that you instantly slow down and hand the victory over to someone else. You don't even place in the top three. I just didn't feel as if I should be the one to win. There have been countless other moments of handing over a win because I felt I wasn't supposed to have victories. Of course, at the time, I didn't articulate these feelings and thoughts as beliefs of worthlessness. Subconsciously, I didn't feel I was good enough.

The beliefs I had about myself were set in motion through my early childhood trauma of molestation. At the time, I didn't realize those traumatic events had any affect over me. I had internalized those events, somehow believing it was my fault. Something had to be wrong with me to have these things happen to me. It wasn't until I begin to look over my life and the decisions I made, that I discovered a little girl pretending to be strong. Pretending to be in control. We've heard the stories of women being promiscuous because of their early childhood experiences dealing with molestation. I was no different. I enjoyed the attention from the opposite sex, but I didn't always enjoy what came with the attention. Don't get me wrong there were moments where I wholeheartedly wanted to engage in sexual activity. However, there were those that left me feeling like I had no other choice than to take control and "give" them what they wanted before they "took" what they wanted. One incident occurred with a man in his twenties when I was only fourteen years old. In my mind we would just hang out and have fun. Fun led to him forcing himself on me and after a series of "Nos" from me, he continued to force his will. I remember feeling dirty and ashamed and at fault. From that moment forward, I subconsciously decided no one would ever "take" my body. If I ever found myself in those sorts of situations, I'd just "give" myself to him. This made me feel like I was in control.

My lack of self-worth manifested in every area of my life including friendships, school and various opportunities. As a student, I had the potential to be an honor student, yet I did just enough to get by. I felt I wasn't supposed to be a part of the Honor Club. I only made friends with people who pursued me as a friend. I never initiated relationships because I couldn't imagine anyone wanting to hang out with me. I wasn't nearly cool enough or pretty enough. As for opportunities, many times I was offered positions of leadership and would back away because I didn't believe I could succeed. Apparently, people around me could see my potential and the gifts that had been placed inside of me, but I had yet to realize my own value.

All the things I mentioned didn't really seem like much to me. In fact, I typically blew them off as no big deal. I summed all the events up as proof that I just needed to be better, to fix things and make things right. I became a perfectionist, needing things to be just right in order to move forward. I attempted to control every aspect of my life and if I couldn't control the situation or if I didn't know the outcome, I wouldn't move forward. Some call this analysis paralysis. My need for perfection was a natural evolution of my belief that I was not good enough. This need to control and perfect things around me led to an unforgettable anxiety attack in late 2017. Prior to this attack, I had started the journey of discovering me. Starting a business a few years prior, led me to become a better version of myself in order to lead my team. This led me to identifying my feelings of inadequacy in the role of leading a team. I couldn't understand why I wasn't growing as fast as others, why it was such a hard climb for me.

The truth of the matter was I wasn't ready to lead. As my development continued, I began to identify a pattern of self-sabotage and lack of confidence. I knew this was a part of my purpose, yet I didn't believe in my heart the things God said about me. I had allowed all those unfortunate circumstances to dictate who I was and what I was worth. My past circumstances created thoughts and images of me that took over my mind like a pack of squatters. Google dictionary defines squatter as, "a person who unlawfully occupies an uninhabited building or unused land." These thoughts had unlawfully occupied my mind!

The turnaround really began to take shape when I started my business. In the beginning, I had to work on myself in order to succeed. As I searched for ways to succeed, I begin to discover myself. My journey of entrepreneurship caused me to become a better version of myself. I begin to read books in my areas of weakness. But that wasn't enough for me, it was a starting point. You see God was drawing me closer and closer to Him. As I learned more of who I was in the present and how I had allowed my past to stunt my growth, I realized the true solution was in my relationship with God. Isn't it funny that many of my struggles were in the area of relationships and here I found my solution, in a relationship. Not any ordinary relationship but one that would cause me to truly learn the meaning of walking by faith and having real joy and peace. God wasn't new to me at this point. I began my walk with God in high school. However, I never allowed Him to lead. God has always been there even though I didn't really know Him. I didn't always recognize or acknowledge His hand. However, He was always present.

I love the Bible story about Joseph. He experienced some extremely horrible situations from being sold off by his brothers to being lied on by his boss's wife and thrown into prison. In each situation his faith remained locked onto the promises of God for his life. He didn't focus on the current situation. He used his gifts in every part of his journey and allowed his gift to make room for him, placing him in his divine purpose. I relate to this story because as I look back over my life, I recognize God's hand in every situation. Not only did I survive each one of those horrible moments but each one played a significant role in my daily transformation to becoming exactly who God called me to be, my divine design.

So how does one escape such an ingrained belief system of feeling worthless? For me it was a matter choosing faith. Faith that through Him, I AM a NEW creation. I remember when my mom stood over me during my anxiety attack and told me I had to choose. I had to choose whether I wanted to come out of this thing or stay right there. That anxiety attack was a gift. It broke me! I learned to fight the battle of purpose.

Your purpose is not going to be handed to you on a silver platter. You cannot lay down and allow things to happen TO you. You must fight. I'm not talking about a physical fight but mentally pressing through the hard times. You must be intentional. Intention starts in the heart and mind. Hence, you must renew your mind with the Word of God. Who does God say you are!! Not who your circumstances say you are because those are just lies that we believe. It wasn't until I identified scriptures of promises and purpose and internalized them, that I began to believe that I AM WORTHY! Like the story of Joseph, I have learned to stand on the promises of God. Not focusing on the situation but choosing to put my focus on God and His divine purpose for my life.

About the Author

Jamela Johnson, a native of Dayton, Ohio, is a wife, mother of five, grandmother of two, educator, entrepreneur and member of The Delta Sigma Theta Sorority, Inc. She received a Bachelor of Arts degree in economics from Wright State University and a Master of Arts in education with a concentration in mild to moderate intervention specialist K-12 from McGregor University.

During seventeen years as an educator, Jamela had the opportunity to inspire adolescents to see possibility and self-worth in the most unfortunate circumstances. During her commission as an educator, Jamela discovered her passion for helping others realize they have already been equipped with the necessary tools to fulfill their God-given purpose.

Jamela is driven by her purpose of helping others become the best version of themselves through sharing her every day journey of self-transformation.

Contact Jamela at BeingJamela365@JamelaJohnson.com or call (937) 380-2960.
FB: @BeingJamela365
IG: @BeingJamela365

Juanita Harris

The Beatitudes of a Widow Queen

Today the Lord instructed me to write about the experience of widowhood from the perspective of the beatitudes. Suspecting this study is more for my growth and reflection, I enter into this with fear and excitement. Fear in terms of the meaning of respect for the wisdom of God concerning my life. Excitement because I have never been disappointed by what God has called me to do. What are my qualifications for being called a widow? For forty-one years I was someone's wife; queen of my household to my husband and king. All of a sudden, in one day I became a widow. There was an identity crisis. Who is this person? A widow was an older woman, with gray hair and reading glasses. I do have gray hair and reading glasses, but I was not the person I saw in my mind's eye.

I Timothy 5:9 tells me who I am:

NKJV: 9 *Do not let a widow under sixty years old be taken into the number, and not unless she has been the wife of one man,*

One month after my husband's death I turned sixty. As often as I've read and heard the New Testament, I had never seen that verse. But it never pertained to me as it does now.

Who I should be is given in I Timothy 5:5:

NKJV: 5 *Now she who is really a widow, and left alone, trusts in God and continues in supplications and prayers night and day.*

The widow in this passage has no children or grandchildren to care for her. The passage is stating the responsibility of the church to take care of her physical needs. No matter our plight, we all need to trust God and pray. For a new season has come, a winter season, cold as snow and sometimes harsh as a wilderness.

Blessed are the poor in Spirit

To lose a beloved spouse causes one to enter a new spiritual realm. No longer do we have the person who knew us intimately. No longer do we walk proudly as the wife of…

You could say our spirits were one. The Apostle Paul said that for a married person their primary cares are for their husband or wife, but for a single person the primary care is for the things of God. My spirit had become poor by one. In essence, the two who became one was torn apart.

My focus will be from the perspective of a widow, because I have only been a widow, and life without a husband is different than life without a wife. I believe one of the reasons for this study is because of my constant concern for financial matters. My husband did not leave me financially well off. I know God is my source and my provider but having never experienced poverty causes me to have to struggle to rest in the provision of my Father. This is my failing not God's failing to provide. Although I am not destitute, I still worry that I'll have enough, and that is not God's will.

There is, however, a poor spirit, a humble and unpretentious spirit. What is more humbling than to be stripped of your covering? To not have the one who protected you from the world and sometimes from yourself. Although God does these things, as humans we often look to other humans for the things that God provides to us in the spiritual realm. Now is the time to know the spiritual is more powerful than the natural. Heaven is my real home and my prayer remains, "Thy will be done on earth as it is in heaven." This becomes more real to me each day. In heaven the angels do not question God, they just glorify Him all the time. In heaven, God is the only focus. God's angels don't experience problems, death, sickness, poverty or marriage to distract them from their purpose, which is to praise the Lord. It is also our purpose.

To humble myself is my will. Some people are humbled by life's situations and some of us must humble ourselves. We perform acts of humility in order to do God's will in our lives. We are independent, self-willed, and self-centered in our carnal selves. Only because of the Lord Jesus Christ in us, can we do the will of God.

Ours is the kingdom of heaven. In the kingdom of heaven, we are comforted, provided for, protected and loved by God. We can love Him without concerns about what others will think. We can pour out our deepest hurts and concerns to Him without being ridiculed. He will not reject us in our time of need. He's only a prayer away. We can serve Him, and He will not mistreat us. We can give Him our all without the fear of being abused. In the kingdom of heaven, we praise, worship and glorify God unashamed. Let it be done on earth as it is in heaven.

Blessed are they who mourn, for they shall be comforted.

Mourning is something we do alone. No matter how many people are around or how close you may be to others, no one can mourn for you. Each person mourns in a different way. Some cry and faint, some seem emotionless; however, we do mourn. Mourning is to feel or express grief or sorrow. For some, we feel more grief than for others who pass away. The first days of my husband's death were busy, and I was numb. I didn't have to feel anything because I was too busy taking care of details. That was my comfort zone and I could keep my mind focused on what I needed to do. Then there are the alone times, the quiet times when no one calls comes by and you are completely alone. It is then we have time to think about our beloved and the little things: the wedding band he gave to me, his fragrance, holding his hand, how he laughed, and so many other little things. Some days are overwhelming and if I don't fix my mind on my Lord Jesus and take it of what I have lost, I would go crazy.

My comfort is hope. My hope that is my husband is at peace and in the presence of the Lord Jesus. I find comfort having spent forty-one years with him and that's worth a lot. I think of the good times and forget about the hard times and there were hard times. I think about what he would say in certain situations and I think I know what he would have said. The comfort in knowing a person so intimately that you know what they would say or think is very comforting. My relationship with God is such that I want to know what He thinks or would say about situations in my life. Meditating on His word gives me insight into what God thinks. I'm not always right just as I was not always right as to what my husband was thinking, but it's comforting to believe you know someone so well. We can never know any one so well that we always know what they think. It's even less likely we will know all of God's thoughts since His thoughts are above our thoughts.

<u>Blessed are the meek for, they shall inherit the earth.</u>

The meek are those who quietly submit themselves to God. I accept this season of my life. Now that I must do everything myself, each day is a physical and emotional challenge. I have no excuse for not spending time with God. This is a season for just me and my Lord. He eats with me and sleeps with me, and oh, how He loves me.

Blessed are they who hunger and thirst for righteousness, for they shall be satisfied.

Fasting from food for a period of time to seek the Lord for His will in your life and the life of the body of Christ can show us how to hunger for God. When I take my mind off of what I'm going to eat next, it is an opportunity to seek what God has for me to eat next. His living water has quenched my thirst so often for those things that cause me to want more and still feel unsatisfied. Shopping is fun but I have limited resources. And even if I were a multibillionaire, things cannot fill the place where a relationship should be, whether with a man or with God. I can only speak for myself, but I do feel good when I shop. God, however, has provided me His word, where I can poke around as much as I want, and it doesn't cost me anything but time. I can chew on the meat of His word for hours and be full of the Spirit when I leave the table. The only thing I gain is satisfaction. My glucose doesn't go up. There are no carbohydrates to turn to sugar and no fat to clog my arteries. I've eaten just to be eating and the miserable feeling afterward was not what I was after. Let God prepare a table before you in the presence of your enemies of loneliness, depression, and extended grief.

Blessed are the merciful, for they shall obtain mercy.

Grief may cause us to be short with those we love and others around us. Our cup of mercy may be half full. The anger part of grieving may linger a bit too long. We're mad at the world because things aren't as good as they were. We have no one with whom to share our daily frustrations and triumphs. My husband, Richard, and I were merciful to each other on a daily basis. That's how you stay married. Have mercy on each another. Of course, it doesn't work that way with God because He doesn't need our mercy. But as He sees our hearts and the mercy we are willing to give each other, He can shower us with renewed mercy every morning.

Blessed are the pure of heart, for they shall see God.

Who are the pure of heart? Can a broken heart be pure? Yes, when we continue to trust and seek God even through our brokenness. God is the comforter and healer of our hearts. Our hearts are being healed as we trust God even more and see Him everywhere.

Blessed are the peacemakers, for they shall be called the children of God.

My idea of a peacemaker is someone who keeps the peace at all cost. Not so in the kingdom of God. A peacemaker makes things peaceful. We cannot make anything peaceful until we are peaceful. If our insides are turned upside down, we can only cause turmoil and strife. But when we go to "The Peace" as we need to go to so often, we can someday give peace to others who go through the stormy days of widowhood.

As a child of God, I can go to Him every day and say, "You know what I need" and He has never disappointed me."

Blessed are they who are persecuted for the sake of righteousness for theirs is the Kingdom of Heaven.

Sometimes we may feel persecuted. Maybe it's just me but it seems I don't have very many married friends any more. As a matter of fact, I don't have too many people to call on the phone, including my family. I travel alone, I eat alone, and it seems I have done nothing wrong, but I feel persecuted for the position of being a widow. In this position, I have so much time to go to the kingdom of heaven to talk to my Father. The Bible says the widow is to continue in supplications and prayers night and day. Learning to first visit with the Father before allowing my feelings take me to the land of despair or to the pity party is still an ongoing challenge.

Each day I become better at communicating with my Source and my King Jesus.

About the Author

Juanita is currently pursuing a bachelor's degree in business administration at Southern Illinois University. She expects to pursue a career in a field that will utilize her hard work and accomplishments as a talented and experienced woman of faith. Her goals in life are now on Godly things. On her journey, Juanita has acquired a master's degree in Christian counseling and psychology. As a life group leader and professional life coach, her goal is to reach women who need a partner to walk with for a season and help them reach their highest potential. With more than twenty years of serving in ministry, she continues to share the joy of walking with Jesus.

A widow after forty-one years of marriage with three grown children and two grandchildren, Juanita loves to travel. She has been blessed to travel to Africa, Haiti, and Israel.

Juanita may be contacted by email to juanitah2000@yahoo.com or by phone to (937) 342-0379.

Latrice Hamilton

Empowered by His Love,
Strengthened by His Grace

Born to a teenage mother, fathered by a man unsure whether he could bare the responsibilities of caring for me, statistically, the odds were not in my favor. As a child, the relationship between my biological dad and I was strained. He missed so many of my greatest moments and astounding achievements throughout the years. He missed seeing the fears I came up against and obstacles that challenged me. I learned to forgive him for my sake. I wanted to release the feelings of hurt, rejection and disappointment. Realizing that because I loved all of me, even the part that is my biological dad, it served me no purpose to go on hating him. I forgave him for my very own peace of mind.

Instead, I learned to focus on and appreciate all of the individuals God placed in my life, especially my stepdad, who is my Dad. He has always accepted me as his very own. He believed in me and encouraged me to pursue my educational goals. He pushed me in times when I doubted myself and my abilities.

My mother sacrificed her own dreams and goals to ensure I had everything I needed, and more. Her sacrifice gave me greater determination to succeed and make her proud of the decision she made. To this day, Mom tells the story of how I cried when I was not assigned the longest part in the school play or I when I would cry because I wanted to have all of the answers right for homework, including the bonus questions. I graduated at the top of my high school class with the highest honors and was inducted into the Hall of Fame as one of the top five graduating seniors. My picture remains on the high school wall today.

Honestly, as I grew up, I thought that being pretty meant having long hair and light skin. Here I was with caramel skin and short hair. Oh, how I hated my hair and thought I would die to have long hair like most of my friends. It was not until 12th grade, when I got a really short hairstyle, that I realized that hair did not define my worth and it never has. God loves me regardless of what features I may or may not have.

My value is not defined by my hair, makeup, material things, degrees, status, work ethic, titles, or even other individuals. My worth and value are found in the eyes of God, what I call my "God-Worth." God created us with a purpose and a plan before we were born. When we allow ourselves to focus anywhere else, our view of self becomes distorted. God values you and He loves you.

Growing up in Mississippi, my family orientation was southern Missionary Baptist Church and having a relationship with God is deeply rooted in my history. However, I learned that I had to develop my own personal walk with God to see what his calling on my life would be. On July 3, 2006, the stepping stones to my calling, destined by God, were put into place. I gave birth to my baby boy.

My pregnancy was great. There were no complications and all reports were normal during the entire nine months. Eagerly I awaited the birth of my baby. During labor, my doctors discovered that my baby had an abnormal heart beat. Unconcerned, my excitement continued, and I did not worry at all. Twenty-one hours later, I was rushed to the operating room for an emergency cesarean section. My baby was stressed in the birth canal. Upon delivery, my son was rushed directly to the Neonatal Intensive Care Unit (NICU). I never heard him cry nor was I able to hold him. I only saw his lifeless body briefly, as the doctor rushed out to give him lifesaving cardiopulmonary resuscitation (CPR).

Later, in recovery, one of the doctors reported baby boy had a heart murmur. The NICU doctor was very adamant that there was something more and ordered more testing. She shared with my husband and I her suspicion that our son was having infantile spasms and would need to be transferred to another hospital for more extensive testing. On day three, the NICU doctor said that the test results revealed a stroke on his brain and confirmed what she suspected on his first day of birth, a diagnosis of Tuberous Sclerosis Complex (TSC); a word that sounded like a foreign language to us in its pronunciation and meaning.

The doctor continued to explain that TSC is a rare genetic disorder with no cure. All I heard was that there were "so many brain tumors on his brain that we stop counting, three heart tumors in dangerous places, seizures, and multiple cysts in both kidneys." She also explained that TSC causes developmental delays, learning disabilities, and he may only live to see his first birthday. My heart sunk in that very moment and tears began to flow. How could this be? We were told by the doctors that all we could do at this time was to monitor his progress. I felt broken, defeated, scared, angry, confused, disappointed, and my mind was clouded with so many questions. Denial was my first response. I kept telling myself that he was not having seizures and I tried to convince myself that this was not true.

After being in NICU for two weeks, our son was discharged. As we took him home, I was still living in denial and determined to live a normal family life. After watching my baby have constant, uncontrollable infantile spasms, I came to except the reality that my baby boy was having seizures. I called my mother, crying, asking her to pray for my son. We prayed together. Then she told me, "pray for your son like I have always prayed for you, and God will give you everything you need to care for him." My mother was so RIGHT!

That day, I let my feelings of denial go and stood ready to face TSC head on, no matter what came my way. I thank God every day for my amazing mother and I cherish the relationship we share. I thank her for showing me how to put total faith in God in all situations. You are the best mother and grandmother that a daughter and grandson could ever ask for. We love you and because of your support, I know that God is awesome and with me every step of this journey.

Currently, there is no cure for TSC, but there is still HOPE! My life is living proof of what God can do in your life and how you can find your value and worth in Him. I feel so blessed to see progress in my son's life. I refuse to give up and refuse to take no for answer, even when facing daily challenges and medical complications. There was also an official diagnosis of Autism Spectrum Disorder at age five in support of the diagnosis at eighteen months that our son had autistic features. I decided this diagnosis would not steal my joy and, in my mind, I said, "Bring it on, I am ready to tackle you too."

During this process I was given a choice to stay in my job as a school counselor or to care for my son's needs. I was told that no one would help me like they did. My reply? "I am a child of God and my choice is to always put my son first." I stepped out on faith. God closed one door and opened another one because today, I stand before you as a licensed professional counselor. I know I am blessed and highly favored by Him. I put my trust in God and He never fails. Best decision I ever made! God has made me an example of His goodness even in unexpected circumstances and He always reminds me of how worthy I am. I listened to God's voice saying, "I will assist you; you are not alone, I will give you advantages and bring the right people in your life to bless you in the midst." I believed it and I received it!

Some ask how I do it. Believe it or not, there are days when I cannot imagine our lives without TSC and autism. I am grateful and I continue to smile, embracing every moment. Life is precious and moments are priceless! We have to adapt to changes and accept things as they are and know that God has our back.

At times I will review past medical records that bring out so many memories and emotions. I am reminded of how far we have come. My son's doctor prescribed a new medication called Afinitor. This is a chemotherapy drug, the same medication that cancer patients take. There was no way to deny my feelings. I was scared. I am human and had no idea TSC would lead us here, yet this disease is so unpredictable. He was prescribed this medication to reduce the tumors growing in his little body. Weighing the positives and the negatives, we decided to proceed with the drug. Currently, I have found cognitive improvements from Afinitor and a reduction in the size of tumors. On the day we realized this, it was about to rain, and the clouds were getting dark. As I looked up, I noticed a small glimpse of sunlight helping me to remember that the sun (and the Son) continue to shine upon my life. I am fearfully and wonderfully made!

My son no longer has tumors in his heart, and he experiences some seizure-free days. Rather than demonstrating repetitive speech, we have full conversations. From hitting behavior to hugging, talking out his feelings, and from major meltdowns to an increase in patience, my son has excelled. He has unique acting skills, impeccable memory and amazing video making skills. My parenting style is based on what is best for his needs not based on the standards of other. As a mom, I used to worry about his independent skills as he gets older, but I will not let circumstances defeat me before even trying to conquer them.

Proudly I stand as a special needs mom. You may ask, "Why me?" I ask, "Why not me?" God knew I could handle this special assignment. My life's journey has made me a better person with bold faith, love, patience, acceptance, and understanding. I have gained strength, courage, and confidence in each experience. My fears are calmed, and I gained a clearer perspective once I focused on God's promises. I have so much joy that and I dance and sing in the rain of autism and TSC. No matter what my life has in store, absolutely all things are a blessing.

Exercising has been a positive way to relieve stress and help me stay motivated to keep pushing forward. The caregiver has to take care of herself. I stay fit by strengthening my connection mentally and spiritually. Working out is my therapy. Every day is a good day, regardless. Stay focused and stay in Faith. On a sunny day, traveling through Mississippi, I thought about my grandmother and how she groomed me to be a leader and a lady that stands strong. I can hear her voice telling me "you are going to make it; you are God's child so hold your head up!"

My husband lets me know how valuable I am as a woman to him. I adore him. He has been there every step of the way, never leaving our side. He offers love, support, and encouragement. Dad is our biggest coach and cheers us on during challenging times. He always whispers, "Baby, you got this. I am here with you all the way, no matter what." He allows me to get much needed rest while he cares for our son's needs and makes it a priority to attend the multiple doctors' appointments we schedule. Having a child with medically complex issues can greatly impact any marriage. We communicate, we love, we laugh, we date, we dance, and we are best friends.

Even during the darkest moments, I am thankful for my son's life. There is always something to be grateful for, so I count my blessings. It is not easy, there are hard days and nights, but it has been so worth the fight and I shall endure. Watching my son having a seizure or giving him emergency medications for them to stop never gets easier for me. What I know is that I can do hard things and so can you. I see challenges as opportunities for personal growth. I allow myself to grieve, to feel mad, to feel sad, and to feel scared. Feelings are normal and we don't have to hide them, but don't allow yourself to say stuck there. Rise up in faith and leave fear behind.

Don't pretend it isn't happening, denial is the mask of embarrassment. Deal with the embarrassment and denial in healthy ways. Face it! You are more than an illness, depression, disappointment, anxiety, fear, abuse, and autism. You are an overcomer!

From time to time, I give myself permission to cry. I mean a really good right down ugly cry. For me, it brings peace and relief off of my shoulders. My life's journey is so unique on this daily bumpy road trip of TSC and autism.

Due to the intensity and frequency of seizures, my son has not been able to attend school. He is now being medically monitored through a CBD oil trial study. He has new medications, a diagnosis of high blood pressure, and liver enzymes issues. We are always facing the unpredictable and this has been a ride this go-around. Fortunately, I was given a much-needed break from my career and I am so blessed for my support system. From time to time, I need breaks to renew me (mentally, physically, and spiritually). I learned to ask for help, especially self-care breaks. There is no way I could do this alone. I learned it is okay to ask for help without feeling guilty as a special needs mom. The greatest lesson I learned is that I don't have to be Super Mom and strong all the time. I still find joy and time for myself! I am worthy. I notice the simple pleasures and live my life as if every day is a miracle.

My mission is help other women gain strength, courage, and confidence in each life transition by finding peace, joy, and happiness in their personal journey. Embrace each day, no matter your situation by empowering the inner you. God will not always remove situations from our lives, but He will walk with you right through them. Take refuge in God and hold on tight! He hears your prayers and He cares for you. He has purpose for your pain. Accept that He has something greater and never give up hope. I am a true example of what overwhelming love and support looks like from women pouring into my life. Open up your heart to love and support from others who truly care, it will be worth the rewards. I send a special thank you to all of the supportive women in my life including my mother, mother-in-law, grandmothers, sister, sister-in-law, aunts, close friends, teachers, mentors, therapists, nurses, and doctors.

Now, hold up your head and walk out your life journey with bold faith. You've got this. Believe it! Yes, I am a mother of a child diagnosed with a rare medical illness AND I am so much more. My life's circumstances do not define who I am. I am God's child and I stand on His promises for my life. I am Beloved. I am Beautiful. I am Valued. I am a Winner. I am Worthy and so are you.

About the Author

Latrice Hamilton is a native of Greenville, Mississippi. She is the passionate owner of Inspired Creative Solutions Therapy LLC, where she focuses on treating individuals of all ages diagnosed with autism, depression, medical illnesses, trauma, and stress-related issues. She is the founder of Fitness Wow Factor with Latrice, a fitness group inspired by women. Married to her wonderful husband and the proud mother of one amazing son, Latrice resides in Memphis, Tennessee, with her family. Her passion is inspired by her own personal experiences with her son who has a rare medical condition known as Tuberous Sclerosis Complex accompanied with epilepsy, and autism.

Latrice received a Master of Education degree in counseling from Delta State University and a certificate in behavioral intervention in autism from the University of Massachusetts. Her expertise covers motivational trainings, seminars, and school consultations.

Latrice's life circumstances do not define who she is. She is so much more. She is worthy and so are you. Sometimes the hardest part of your journey is believing you are worthy of the trip!

To schedule a speaking engagement or training, please contact Latrice Hamilton at Lnsccou@yahoo.com or counseling@ics-therapy.com.

Leola Williams

The Devil Can't Steal My Joy

On January 20, 1949, a baby girl was born to Albertha and David Wilkerson in Jacksonville, Florida. I was that child, the fifth to be born. Our parents had eleven children in all, eight girls and three boys. The siblings I grew up with were, Rosa, Deloris, Barbara, Nolan, Mary, Shirley, Zelena, and Diane. Two of the boys died at an early age. One died as an infant and our other brother, Leon, died at age five as a result of being burned while standing near a kerosene heater to get warm. He was hospitalized and eventually died. Leon was a very smart boy, and this was the first tragedy that I remember in our family. We also lost a sister, Zelena, in 2012 to breast cancer.

At about age three, I was hospitalized, and my right kidney was removed. I do not remember much about this other than seeing my family around me while in the hospital. My mother explained to me later that I had a growth on my kidney, and this was the reason for its removal. At age five, I remember going to school with my brother, Nolan, to sit in his class. I do not know how this was arranged, and I assume that I was curious to learn. One day while walking home from school, it was raining. I fell and bruised my knees and I still have that scar today. As my kidney had been removed, I had a very weak bladder. I can recall urinating in my clothes in elementary school as the teacher would not excuse me to go to the restroom. This was most embarrassing. My mother had to advise the school staff that I had a kidney removed and that they should let me go to the restroom when requested. My dear mother, who is now deceased, had cautioned me not to drink a lot of liquids or tea as it would cause an urgency to urinate. I still try to follow her advice today. Yes, the devil tried to kill me at age three, but I still have joy.

While growing up in our family, our dad, Rev. David Wilkerson, was very strict. He was a smart and intelligent man who provided for his large family. He was a preacher, who built the house we were raised in, owned rental property, and worked mostly at a shipyard as a sandblaster. I remember him coming home tired and dirty many days. My mother was a housewife and my dad served in the U.S. Navy for four years. While in the service, he purchased what he called war bonds (savings bonds) and sent them home to our mother. Once he was discharged from the service, he purchased some land and built our three-bedroom frame house. When I reminisce on this, I cannot remember where all of us slept. We were never hungry and ate a lot of rice for dinner. Also, we never had a lack of clothes. Clothes were handed down from one child to the other.

The neighborhood children loved to come to our house. We had a stone and brick fence in front of our house and that seemed to be the meeting place after school and on weekends. As I mentioned before, our dad was a strict disciplinarian. He had a church that he built at the corner of the street down from our house. We were made to go to church and Sunday School every Sunday. If we were not there when our dad got there, he would come back to the house to get us. When we were older, one of our siblings would warn us that dad was coming down the sidewalk. So, we went the back way and beat him back to the church. That was fun. When someone disobeyed his rules and he could not find out who did it, he would line us all up to get a whipping with a belt. I remember our mom speaking up for me and reminding him that I had one kidney and not to whip me too hard. We had one car and sometimes went to the drive-in movie. I do not know where we all sat in the car, but we did. It was very interesting growing up in the Wilkerson household.

My elementary schools were uneventful, except for the times I urinated in my clothes. I attended R. L. Brown Elementary School which was about five blocks from our house. We walked to school during those days. My first grade teacher was Ms. Wilson, who was a good teacher and very nice. My fourth grade teacher, Ms. Leapheart, was very mean. I was a good student and never got into any trouble.

I attended Matthew Gilbert Jr. and Sr. High School, which was located on the next street over from our house. My siblings attended there, too. We could hear the bell ring from our house, and when heard it, we rushed to get to school before the tardy bell rang. I was given favor and was assigned to work in the Dean of Girls Office and the Dean of Boys Office. The Dean of Boys, Mr. Thompson, made a great impression on me as he had a booming voice that one could hear way down the hallway. I was a bit afraid of him but it worked out okay working in his office with his secretary. He was responsible for paddling and suspending the boys. He would often go off campus to get boys from the store and bring them back to the campus. I'm sure that many of the boys, who are now men, remember Mr. Thompson. I was not active in any sports or the band. I joined the yearbook staff as I liked editing and seeing the finished product; I became editor my senior year. I was also inducted into the National Honor Society. As a Superlative in the yearbook, I was chosen for "Best Personality." I graduated third in our class of two hundred students.

Our yearbook advisor was a nice gentleman. I was so involved in the yearbook during my senior year, I remained after school to work on it, along with the advisor. One day, the advisor asked me what I planned to do after high school. I told him that I wanted to become a secretary since I felt my parents could not afford to send me to college. He encouraged me to apply for college at his alma mater, Tuskegee Institute. It is now called Tuskegee University. I had not even heard of Tuskegee. To make a long story short, I applied for admission and was accepted. I had no idea how I would pay for my college, so I applied for financial aid. I was walking on faith. To my surprise, I was awarded a grant. I was accepted to the summer program before enrolling as a freshman. One day, the yearbook advisor and his wife drove up to our house. They wanted to speak to my parents about me. His wife accused me of going with her husband. She questioned why I was staying after school working on the yearbook with him. I denied the charges as I was innocent. I do not know what my parents told them, but they left. I cried many tears over this, as it hurt to be falsely accused. There was no hanky-panky going on, I was just dedicated to doing my job as editor. As a result, I did not attend the summer session.

I enrolled in Tuskegee in the fall. This was my first time being away from home and in a different state. I realized that I was academically unprepared for college as I had not taken college prep classes in high school. I flunked math and had to repeat the class. It was an adjustment period for me, and I had to put my best foot forward, as they say. I decided to major in social work to have a career of helping people. I enjoyed my time there matriculating with Tom Joyner, the radio personality, and the Commodores. In my sophomore year, I became pregnant by my boyfriend in October of 1967. After I told Ralph, the baby's father, that I was indeed pregnant, he wanted no part of it and left school without telling me. I called his father to advise him that I was pregnant by his son. He merely said that he would talk to him and I decided to leave school.

I knew that after three months, pregnancy begins to show, so I went home for the Christmas break and did not return. I was embarrassed, but I had to confess to my mom that I was pregnant. I thought she would scold me or throw me out, but she did not. I told her that I would get a job to help myself before the baby came. I worked as a substitute teacher for a few months. I remember an elementary student patting me on my belly, and she was patting my son in the womb.

After having my baby whom I named Byron, I remained out of school for a year and then returned the following year. My mom agreed to keep the baby for me. Once I returned to Tuskegee, I got back into the swing of things and kept it a secret that I had had a baby. During this time, having a baby out of wedlock was frowned upon. I graduated in May of 1971, with a Bachelor of Science degree. The devil tried to discourage and stop me, but I still have joy!

After graduating from Tuskegee, I returned to Jacksonville to find work. I was hired in November of 1971 as a social worker for the State of Florida. I initially worked with welfare mothers on Aid to Families with Dependent Children, then I worked in Protective Services investigating cases of abuse and neglect. This was hard but rewarding work.

In April of 1977, I married Lafayette H. Williams after dating only about six months. From this union we had three boys, Lafayette, Jr., Langston and Joseph. He adopted my oldest son, Byron. My husband and I married, got divorced and then remarried. It has now been forty years together with our ups and downs but we are now in the marriage for the long haul. Our children are grown, and we have four grandchildren.

In 1985, I obtained a Master of Social Work degree from Florida State University. The instructors came to Jacksonville and taught us in evening classes at the University of North Florida. The State of Florida reimbursed me for the classes I took to earn my degree. Before graduating, I needed a place to intern with the State, but I could not find a suitable place to intern. I accepted a position at the Children's Home Society in Jacksonville., Florida as an adoptions social worker. Part of my duties was to advocate for families to adopt black and biracial children. I appeared on television and spoke at churches and community meetings to recruit families to adopt. This position was the most rewarding of my social work career. I left there after about three years for personal reasons.

Later, I obtained a position at a local nursing home. The employer operated both a hospital and a nursing home. I was asked to accept a position at the nursing home even though I had applied to work at their hospital. So, I took the position at the nursing home. At first, they were glad to have me as I was the only black social worker on staff. Later, I began to have conflict with a Caucasian nurse who wanted to micro-manage me. We had disagreements and did not get along. The job became very stressful and my supervisor inquired why we did not get along. She set up a meeting to discuss our differences, but things did not get any better.

In 2006, my physician was concerned about my lab results and phoned me at work. She said that we needed to find out why my blood levels were so low. She called in a prescription for me for iron pills and scheduled me to come in for an exam. After discovering that I never had a colonoscopy, she referred me out to have one. I went in for the procedure at a local hospital. The physician was very nice to me. When I woke up from the procedure, he advised me that I had colon cancer. All I could do was cry!

My husband was there with me that day to console me and I had to decide what to do. My family was very supportive during this time. I relied on my faith in Jesus, knowing that He would see me through this. I met Linda Hood through a magazine ad. She was an herbalist and I set up an appointment to consult with her. After counseling me, she recommended the four-herb tea. She said that it cures cancer. I got the tea from her and went home to prepare it according to the directions. I began taking the tea and reading scriptures on healing daily.

In the meantime, my physician referred me to a surgeon for possible surgery. I felt that I did not want to have any surgery. A nurse friend of mine, Laveria Dent, (who lives in California) was on our prayer line. She encouraged me to proceed with the surgery. She said that the Lord gives doctors knowledge to help us told me not be afraid as the Lord was with me. I had persons praying for me on our prayer line. I went in for the surgery on November 5, 2007 and remained in the hospital for a week.

When it was time for my discharge, the physician came in to give me a report. He advised that everything went well with the surgery. I asked what the report on my lymph nodes was, and he said that they were clear. This was the news I wanted to hear as I knew that I had been healed. When I returned for my follow up appointment, the surgeon recommended that I take chemotherapy. I rejected this as I was healed in the name of Jesus. He said that if I did not take it that the cancer would return. I told him that I would rather take my chances with Jesus. After recuperating for six weeks, I had to return to work, even though I did not feel up to it. They fired me from that job due to racism. Also, I guess I was too much of a risk after having cancer. Yes, the devil tried to kill me, but I am still here and still having my joy.

I give God the Praise! Why don't you praise the Lord with me!

About the Author

Leola Wilkerson-Williams is a born again Christian, and the author of a children's book called, *How Joseph Met the President,* which is available on amazon.com. She is retired and earned a Bachelor of Science degree in social work from Tuskegee University and a Master of Social Work degree from Florida State University. She is married to Lafayette H. Williams, Sr. and they have four sons, Byron, Lafayette Jr., Langston and Joseph, and have also been blessed with four grandchildren. In addition to writing, she enjoys writing poetry, walking, traveling and being a community activist. She founded the Agape Love Women's Conference in honor of her sister, Zelena Crawford, who died in 2012 from breast cancer. The conference is held annually in May in Jacksonville, Florida. Leola also hosts a prayer line that meets on Monday, Wednesday and Friday from 8 a.m. to 9 a.m. EST. She and her husband reside in her hometown of Jacksonville, Florida. Leola can be reached at williamsleola77@gmail.com.

Loretta Spearman

Identity Buried

When you know who you are, you no longer look to others to tell you and no matter what roadblocks you face, your identity is secure.

It's amazing to see so many struggling with identity crisis. We are told at an early age many things that lie about who we really are, whether it was just joking, teasing, an angry remark, or someone just being plain mean. The effects of these negative words along with many other factors begin to warp and reshape who we are destined to be. Here begins identity theft. Instead of developing into the person you were created to become, you begin to deteriorate and disappear behind all the issues of life. Your confidence, hope and dreams get snatched by disappointments, fears, doubts, assaults and insecurities, to name a few.

Then you begin to agree with the thief with negative self-talk and entertaining negative thoughts.

I want to share my story of how this played out in my life.

Who am I?

I am the oldest of four children and was expected to watch over my siblings and be an example. I had both my parents and lots of aunts and uncles who loved me. I had a pretty good childhood with very little hassle or disruptions, so I thought this was the good life. Everyone told the truth because you aren't supposed to lie about anything. Of course, I learned later that everything is not what it appears to be. As with many families of that era, secrets and cover-ups were the norm. Because of this, I lived in a world of fantasy and not reality. I look back and realized that there was a lot of hidden hurt, pain and disappointments. I was encouraged by my father to succeed in life but wasn't given instruction on how to do that. My father was not slack on encouraging me, but the insecurity and low self-esteem was there, and he didn't know how to help me overcome that. You see, my father never fulfilled his destiny to be his true self because of interferences and sabotages of life.

Because I saw this dream unfulfilled in my dad, it gave me inspiration to push and accomplish what he didn't and that was to get a college degree. I did it for my father, not me! I was happy to complete that goal, but it was not about me. Without even realizing it, I had no dreams or goals in life. When you don't consider yourself worthy or deserving of the benefits of a good life, you tend to sabotage your destiny without even realizing it. You begin to lose yourself. You become what everyone else needs and push yourself further back until *you* disappear.

It seemed my identity crisis began long before I left home at age seventeen to marry with a child on the way. First, I didn't like the color of my skin or my hair texture, nor did I believe anyone could really like me. I put everyone in the viewpoint I had about myself and got a negative observation. You see, I never talked to anyone about what they thought or how I felt, I just perceived incorrectly. I went through life short-circuiting my happiness on incorrect data programmed in my mind.

Here I was in a marriage because of pregnancy, not love, and no clue of what I was about to go through as a teenage wife and mother. Who would I tell that I was being beaten and abused? In my mind, it was all my fault because I chose to marry this man against my parents' counsel. I was ashamed and embarrassed about what was happening to me and didn't really understand it all. I saw no way out but to just take the abuse. We have no idea how being abused can affect how we see ourselves. It was naïve not to reach out and tell the parents who had always taken good care of me. I had no dreams or goals; I began to accept this as my fate in life. I believe this began the process of my identity slipping away. I began to turn inward and hide myself from the reality I was living so I could survive.

Escapism

One way we lose self is through escapism. We don't look at or deal with the issues that plague us. Instead we get involved in everything that takes us away from that reality: drinking, sex, overeating, or an obsession with anything that makes us forget. I partied and didn't allow myself to think or feel. The problem with this is you make the same mistakes over and over. You find yourself in a cycle that keeps repeating itself and you keep going around that same mountain. By then your pattern of thinking has become set in a manner that leaves no room for healing and experiencing a better life. Romans 12:2 "And do not be conformed to this world but be transformed by the renewing of your mind, so that you may prove what the will of God is, that which is good and acceptable and perfect."

Coming out of that first marriage left me with toxic thoughts and a hardened heart. I was conforming to the world in my thinking. Needless to say, I ended up marrying two more times. The second marriage was to a misogynist who threatened to take my life, but God's grace was upon me. You see God has a purpose and a plan for you. The third marriage was to a kind and caring man, but he had his own issues that clashed with mine. Once again, I saw all the red flags but ignored them and it could have cost me my life. When God finally got my attention, I asked why I married men who physically, mentally, and sexually abused me. How could this happen? None of these men were like my father, who I adored. I was perplexed and dismayed for making bad choices, not once but three times. Well, God answered, and it wasn't what I expected.

I was told the problem was me! I cried as I begin to see how true that answer was and how I had totally lost my identity. I had allowed the cares of life to literally destroy Loretta. All I went through in the one marriage stripped me and it continued through every relationship I engaged in because my hope was gone, and fear was in its place. I had lost sight of life itself. It was only about taking care of my two daughters and working every day with a little self-indulgence whenever I could grab it.

Loved

The second thing that kept me from knowing me was love. I didn't like me let alone love me. I begin to discover that first, I had no clue about love. I had said it multiple times, but it was never in my heart. You see, I placed a wall around my heart to keep from being hurt again after the first marriage. So, I thought if the man says he loves you and wants to be with you, why not? I entered marriages without understanding who I was and it was for all the wrong reasons. The second commandment says; "You shall love your neighbor as yourself." When that love is missing, you will consume one another. You lose sight of who God created you to be and delay your destiny. I say delay because God is ready and willing to bring you to that place of your true identity. Psalm 139:16 "You saw me before I was born and scheduled each day of my life before I began to breathe. Every day was recorded in Your book." You were born with a purpose and a plan. Somewhere the cares of the world infiltrate the process and takes us off course. I heard someone say, delay is not denial. The fact that you recognize what the issue is lets you know that you're ready to move forward.

My turnaround came when I turned forty. I met the Holy Spirit in Detroit, Michigan, at Dr. Keith Butler's church, while visiting my friend. It changed my life and my vision. As I allowed the Holy Spirit to lead me, I began to see my past, my present and my future. I began to finally see who the real me was and I was so thankful that my life was being restored. As I went through the process of finding me, I married for the third time before the Holy Spirit could complete the process and ended up in a marriage that was never meant to be, thereby creating turmoil for me and my husband. During this third marriage I began to see myself realizing that I should have waited but my flesh was still holding on to self-indulgence. But I was determined to uncover who I really was created to be in this life.

As my identity was uncovered, it was revealed that I was a leader, I was an equipper, a preacher, an administrator, and a prophet. I became a better mother and a grandmother. I graduated from college and graduate school, became a certified belief counselor. I have compassion now and my failures and fears no longer imprison me. My identity is a plethora of qualities that I had no idea were waiting to surface.

As your identity resurfaces and you face those insecurities and low self-image, you are able to recognize the entrapments that made you compromise, justify, or ignore the red lights. No longer are you attempting to be someone else but you appreciate who you are. You are satisfied and complete. You are here today in spite of obstacles, criticisms, rejections and mockery. Each day you get up with purpose and thanksgiving because you overcame all odds and endured the storms of disappointments and discouragement. You are a living testimony!

You don't have to settle for mediocrity! Take time to appreciate you. Learn more about you and revive those dreams and inspirations that were buried but not dead. You don't have to measure yourself to others. You are a unique design. Stop comparing yourself with others and be who you were called to be whether it's a secretary, a chef, architect, or nurse; it doesn't matter. Learn to recognize your strengths and that which brings you joy. Find your passion, fuel it and enjoy the process. Take time to uncover the real you and allow those treasures within to be revealed.

I want you to repeat these confessions daily:

I am blessed and full of joy.

I have been created to prosper and succeed no matter what I face today.

I am filled with the Peace of God.

My vision is clear and filled with purpose.

My eyes are opened to see and my ears are opened to hear what the Spirit of God is saying to me.

I am fruitful because God's plans are working in me.

I am not anxious about anything because my trust is in God.

Prayer

Father God, I thank you for waking me up to who you created me to be. Without you it couldn't have happened. Thank you for loving me when I didn't love myself. Thank you for restoring me and healing me of insecurities and toxic thoughts that held me captive. I am excited to see all that you have planned for my journey. I trust you and lean not to my own understanding because you know me, and I come into agreement with your plans. I give you all the praise and glory for the greater works that you have deposited in me that will be pleasing in your sight. In Jesus's Name.

About the Author

Elder Loretta McCalister-Spearman, a prophet of God, a mother of two daughters (son-in-law), and seven grandchildren resides in Dayton, Ohio. Loretta has a passion to see people set free to be all that God has called them to be in this lifetime. She has authored a healing and deliverance manual and teaches on spiritual warfare. Her vision is to see people equipped, trained and armed to resist, take back and overcome the forces of evil; to help them recover the dreams and purposes that were stolen and hijacked.

Loretta has a bachelor's degree in human resource management from Capital University, a master's degree in Christian education and counseling from the International Apostolic College of Grace and Truth. She is a certified biblical counselor, and a certified belief therapist. You can contact Loretta by email to tarry2u@gmail.com or by phone at (937) 321-1783.

Mel Roberson

Air...Earth...Water...Fire

Pinkie Liggons was the youngest of 10 children, and she was born a fighter.

Her father was part of the Tuskegee Syphilis Experiment down in Tuskegee, Alabama. I've been told that her one of her brothers was part of it, too. African-American men were injected with syphilis and not given treatment. Pinkie Liggons was the youngest of 10 children, and she was born a fighter. Even though she had a gentle spirit, she was strong willed and confident. I guess it was necessary to be that way in the South during the early 1900s if you wanted to survive. It must have been hard to watch your family members die for the sake of an experiment that was more like genocide. Even though times were difficult, she always kept her head to the sky.

Pinkie became the "Air" of her family. She was a free-spirited thinker. Her positive attitude made her a joy to be around. She had a smile that could light up a whole room. I had the privilege of knowing her... she was my great grandmother. Her life in Tuskegee set the stage for what she would become, and what she would teach her children. She would teach her four offspring to have a great work ethic, to be flexible, to stay positive, and to always have faith. Not only would she teach that to her children, but to her grandchildren and great grandchildren as well.

One of her four children was Thelma Peters. Born in Alabama, Thelma later moved to Chicago and had six children of her own. Thelma was the "Earth" of her family. She was the foundation... solid as a rock. She had unshakable character. I had the opportunity to know her as well... she was my grandmother. Though earth has characteristics that are solid, it also provides fertile ground that can spring forth a wonderful harvest. Thelma had wonderful food for thought. She would often tell us "If you don't have a horse, ride a mule." I'm sure that her insightful sayings were influenced by her mother, Pinkie. Thelma taught us to be strong and face adversity head on. She had to raise children when civil rights didn't exist. Her strength, along with her mom's flexibility, was passed on to her children. Thelma was the second oldest of her brothers and sisters. Out of the six children that Thelma had, Danella Roberson was the second to be born.

A Chicago native, Danella would take trips to the South in her youth and enjoy picking watermelons from the watermelon patch on her family's land. Danella would take the tenacity and diligence of the

South and couple that with the creativity and certitude of the North. She was born creative. Danella became the "Water" of her family. She was soothing, yet strong enough to smooth out stone. Water can be soothing. It can also be powerful enough to wipe out a city. Danella possessed the ability to move around any problem or situation that got in front of her. Born in the mid-1940s, she witnessed the abuse that African Americans took as they fought for equal rights. I know this to be true because she is my mother.

The women in my family have been the caregivers. They have been the ones to record and teach our family history. They have been the ones to plant the seeds of greatness in us. Though my mom had no daughters to pass the "Queen's Legacy" to directly, she gave my brother and I the tools necessary to start us on the road to success. (My father's story will be told at another time.) The wisdom of the ages has been passed from generation to generation in my family. My mom's fluid-like capabilities showed my brother and I that power doesn't have to come from force. She exemplifies gentleness, being able to get the job done.

Fortunately, my mother does have the chance to teach a princess how to be queen. My two daughters enjoy spending time with my mother. My girls are my "Fire." They keep my heart warm. They are passionate and enthusiastic. They demonstrate strength. Many people think of the destructive characteristics of fire, but fire also represents action, passion, desire, and protection. My oldest daughter made the varsity cheerleading team as a freshman. She was the captain of the team by her sophomore year. My youngest daughter was born earlier than expected and has kept doing everything in life early. She walked at nine months, talked in complete sentences by two years old, and used words like "extremely" and "cooperative" by the time she was three.

I'm happy to be a prince in the kingdom of my family. Though the queens around me represent different characteristics of the elements, they all work together for the greater good of our noble clan. Now that I think about it, they all possess a little of each element. It has been a blessing to learn from all of the women in my life. When God made the world, all the elements were put here to create balance. I'm happy He thought enough of my family to create that same balance for us.

About the Author

Mel Roberson is an accomplished speaker, actor, spoken word artist, poet, author and model. For more information or to contact Mel Roberson, visit www.melrobentertainment.com.

Mkale Warner

Are You Your Mother's Child?

I heard a true story about a three-legged dog that had puppies. The dog walked with a limp because she only had three legs and when the puppies were born, they were in perfect health and had all four legs. Yet, because they grew up around their mother and watched her walk with a limp, the puppies who stayed with the mom also walked with a limp. They did what they saw their mother do, because they believed it was normal.

As a child I always watched my mother and wanted to imitate everything she did. She was real and authentic. I loved everything about her. She would stand up for people who were less fortunate and was always advocating for some cause. I saw my mom work hard and love even harder. Tiny in stature, I thought my mom was superwoman and I prayed that one day I would live up to the example she showed me.

But I guess I didn't pray nearly enough. Pregnant at seventeen, dating a drug dealer, and on my way to jail was a far cry from what my mom taught me. However, loving the wrong man was a lesson I learned from her. There were no lectures or books to read on "how to love the wrong man," I simply mastered what I saw. I watched my mom struggle with most of her relationships. She gave herself completely to someone, never really getting anything back in return. That practice became part of my normal.

They say generational curses get stronger with each generation. I was evidence of that. On a chilly September evening, my curse made its appearance, and it sent federal agents to collect. The FBI came looking for me and my then boyfriend. They captured him and I hid under a bush. It was there I made "my deal with God." I promised God that if He protected me, I would never do anything with illegal drugs again. I was facing federal charges that could have changed the trajectory of my life and somehow, by the grace of God and the prayers of my parents, I walked away never seeing the inside of a jail cell.

I kept my promise to God. I decided to attend Bible college. After I gave birth to my oldest daughter, Jimmerlyn, we were on our way to pursue my degree and begin a new life. It was no small feat. It was tough being a single mother in a Bible college. But I had the support of my family and I wanted to completely turn my life around, which was my end of "my deal with God." After college, I married and had more two children, Kayla and Kaylee. I was entering full-blown mommy mode and of course, because superwoman was the goal, I needed to be an amazing business woman as well. So, when my mom wanted to start a mortgage company, it was the perfect scenario. I could be at home with my children, take care of my family and still have my own business.

She and I were like magic. She was the visionary of the company and I was the vision executor. There were days when my mom would come into the office, without sleep and work like she had eight hours of rest and a Red Bull. This would go on for weeks at a time. I could not understand why I did not have her energy levels, especially being half her age. But then I thought, she was superwoman after all, and maybe I would get my superpowers later in life.

Conversely, my mom would also have moments when she was sick for weeks at a time. It was almost like she had a constant flu. What she went through didn't make sense to me, but I assumed it would all work out over time. We had the mortgage company for about five years. Even though we were doing well, I eventually made the hard decision to take on a traditional job so I could have insurance for my family. So, I left the company and went to work for Lehman Brothers.

Soon after leaving, I understood the cause of my mother's superwoman syndrome. I was in tears on the phone, sitting under the stairs at work talking to a first responder. "Do you want us to take her to the hospital?" he asked. In the background I could hear my mother screaming, "No Mkale! Don't let them take me!"

They called it a 72-hour hold. I had never heard that term before. It was one of the scariest decisions I had to make. I didn't want my mom mad at me, but I was scared if I didn't do something drastic, I would lose her. I made the decision to have them take her to the hospital, and I left work to meet her them there.

She was diagnosed with bipolar disorder. Her moments of what I called superwoman, followed by the flu were actually episodes of being manic and depressed. All the overtime hours, the sacrificing of herself for her family, led to this. I had watched her intently. I had learned to be a great mom, an incredible nurturer—putting everyone else's needs before my own. At first glance these are all great characteristics, but in hindsight, this was another generational lesson to be learned about the lack of self-care.

They say when it rains, it pours. In addition to my mother's disorder, my sweet Kaylee, who was about seven years old and had been diagnosed with epilepsy at six months of age, was also beginning to change. What we did not know was that she had Dravet Syndrome, which also meant that most anti-epileptic medications would not work for her. In fact, they would have an adverse effect on her. On many trips to the doctor there were always a new medication that worked for someone else. However, when we tried it, it was an epic fail. Instead of helping her, she experienced the worst side effects, including severe brain damage and losing her ability to walk. So, I had my mother's bipolar disorder on one side, and my daughter battling an awful disease on the other side. That is when my superwoman mode kicked in. I worked a full-time job, volunteered at church, was a wife, and caregiver to my daughter, my mom and my other two daughters.

And then as if that was not enough life happened again.

Have you ever placed all your eggs in one basket? I did. I woke up to realize that my one basket was my job. I was on the 40/40/40 plan. The plan where you work forty hours per week, for forty years, and you're supposed to be able to retire and live off forty percent of your income. Great plan in theory, but totally ineffective when your company, I won't mention any names (Cherry Creek Mortgage), goes out of business. I started working for Cherry Creek Mortgage after leaving my job at Lehman Brothers. I had just boarded a plane, heading home from a conference, when I received a call from the president of the company. He said, "When you come back you will not have a job. We are closing our doors." The 40/40/40 plan had officially left the building.

For a moment panic set in. But then I thought, "We will be okay. We have a savings account, a 401k, we will be fine." I shook off the shock and went to work setting up my company and became an independent contractor doing mortgages as well as consulting. Things were beginning to look up and then came "the closing."

I was sitting in a title company after my client had finished signing paperwork, waiting for the loan to fund. Our celebratory laughter came to a screeching halt when the closer at the title company walked back into the room and said, "this loan is not funding." "Excuse me, what?" We had done everything they asked us to do and met all the criteria. "What do you mean it's not funding?" I uttered. She looked me square in the eye and said that while we were signing the paperwork the mortgage company closed its doors.

I sat there, at a loss for words. It was happening again. It was like déjà vu. My heart raced out of my chest. Now, I truly began to panic. Our savings were dwindling and my little girl's health was declining. I was running out of options and solutions. I thought, "Oh my God, what am I going to do now?" I drove home in silence, shackled in uncertainty.

Not too long afterward, I got the kids off to school and laid down to have a quick nap. There was so much pressure on me. I remember saying with an audible voice as I lay on my bed "surely, today will be the day that I die." I could not go one step further. Not because I wanted to kill myself, but because I did not know how I could keep breathing while we were losing everything.

The moments came and went, and I was still alive. From there I began my own therapy sessions. I started going to the gym and I gained an insatiable appetite for books on personal development and building wealth. I would be on the recumbent bike and reading at the same time. It was as if the words on the pages of those books were breathing new life into me.

I wish I could tell you things got better from there, but they didn't. I found myself bankrupt, in the middle of an ugly divorce, a single parent with three children (one that required 24-hour care) and not a dime to my name. I had gone from making well over six figures, to barely scraping by on $2,000 a month, and no plan on how I would move forward.

As I began to rebuild my life, I also began to rebuild my mindset, and my personal relationship with myself. I took classes on how to take care of *me*, something I had never done before. At one of the classes, while going through my ugly divorce, someone said to me, "you look like you are in love." I was, but not with another man. I had fallen in love with me.

In my life, I put all my efforts into relationships with God, men, my children, and even my mother. Yet, the one relationship I had never cultivated was the relationship with myself. I began to sing love songs to *me,* I begin to work on *my* emotional, physical, financial and spiritual health. I wanted to be whole. In the midst of this process of learning to love me, I did fall in love with a man, my husband, Kwame, who is now the love of my life. But it was a direct result of me falling in love with *me*.

I have gone back and had some hard discussions with my girls and even apologized to them. I apologized for my bad decisions and for teaching them to take care of everyone but them. I no longer have the desire to be superwoman because I now know the true cost of that title, and it is way too expensive for me. My sweet Kaylee has been in heaven now for three years, but her life remains one of my greatest examples. She lived unapologetically, and I have learned to do the same.

As a woman, I was taught to be all things to all people. I saw an incredible, beautiful brave woman in my mom who could do anything. My mom is still an amazing woman, it just looks very different. I often wonder, had my mother learned to take care of herself would her life have turned out different. Nevertheless, I am grateful for the beautiful and sometimes hard lessons she taught me.

Today my husband and I travel all around the world helping people build wealth and take control of their financial future. When I speak, I often include my thoughts about women, who we are, and how we show up for everyone else except ourselves.

When we travel and the flight attendant goes through the emergency procedures, he or she will include, "if the oxygen mask drops and you are traveling with an infant, put your mask on first before you put the mask on the child." I have learned that the hard way. If you do not apply the oxygen to you first, you will not be alive to take care of those that need you. In many unique ways, my mother taught valuable lessons about a woman's worth. I am my mother's child.

About the Author

Mkale has been an entrepreneur for more than nineteen years. She has owned and operated everything from retail stores to real estate investment companies.

Mkale chose entrepreneurship as a means to be at home to raise her three daughters, one of which had special needs. Leaving Corporate America, she entered the real estate industry as a mortgage broker and a house flipper. In the course of one year, she has closed over $48,000,000 in real estate deals. Her dedication to the industry and commitment to help people win have always shown through in her business ventures.

She is a purpose-driven, trusted leader who prides herself in pouring her heart into her clients. Mkale speaks internationally, educating people about wealth-building strategies in real estate and crypto currency. She is a creative solutionist who offers unique, dynamic tools to the solopreneurs, empowering them to succeed in every area of life.

Mkale is committed to the youth and future of America. She created a wealth-building course using real estate to educate and support them in generating income while gaining real experience investing in real estate.

She is a powerful role model as a woman, entrepreneur, leader, wife and mother. Mkale Warner has created success, balance, and healthy relationships in business, as well as her personal life. You definitely want this woman in your corner!

Contact Mkale by visiting www.womenwealthandcrypto.com, by emailing info@womenwealthandcrypto.com or by phone at (720) 669-4879.

Myesha Miller

The Devil Can't Steal My Joy

We met when I was seventeen and working at a fast food restaurant; he came in to order. He tried to talk to me and gave me his number. In my mind, I was really not interested but didn't care because at this point in my life, I was talking to different guys at the same time anyway. Adding his number to the bunch was nothing to me. When he left the store that day, I made sure to take notice of what kind of car he got into. Turns out it was a Mercedes Benz, and it was customized. A few dates with this man turned into the craziest and most dangerous four years of my life.

He was nine years older than me. Even though it didn't matter to me, I did know not to tell my parents about him. How did I go on dates without my parents knowing? Lie. Lie about who I was with and where I was going. I was working, so when I had new clothes it didn't raise any red flags. It didn't take long before I was having sex with him and found out he was selling drugs. I naively thought that because I had a job and wasn't selling drugs, it didn't concern me. Little did I know a few short years later that would be far from true. Eventually my parents found out about him. I couldn't keep getting away with lying. How did they find out? They asked questions. I was a bad liar and the truth always came out.

My mother told me that a man that old dating someone my age only wanted one thing from me. She wasn't wrong but I didn't care. The thrill of being with an older guy and being showered with gifts, meals, and cash overshadowed the unknown danger I was in. What really sealed it was when I came home to get ready for work and my mom saw the car I was driving. She asked who the car belonged to. When I told her it was my boyfriend's, she—and this was not the first time—went off on me. She told me to never see him again and to take his car back to him. While crying my eyes out, I returned the car and told him what my parents said. He took me home and attempted to talk to my parents. They let him know that he had no business with me, and they did not want us to continue seeing each other. That didn't stop us. My mother didn't want to lose me. When she was the same age, she was pregnant with me and was kicked out of the house.

Years later, I understood their fear. Whether it was the best decision or not, they wanted me near them, and since I was so close to graduating it was even more important for me be at home. During this time, I also was sleeping with another older man I had met. We had a connection, but in my mind, it wasn't anything as serious.

A person can be raised right and given all the right tools. If their mindset is messed up, none of that matters. I deluded myself to believe that what I was doing was okay. Besides, I was young and I wouldn't be like this forever. Thinking that the consequences of bad decision making won't catch up with you nor will they have a long-term effect, even if they do, is a trap in itself. This is not just a story of a part of my life, but it is also the story of many women who willingly turn their lives upside down for the sake of a man.

After I graduated high school, my family moved to another city in Florida. They thought a side benefit of the necessary move was not dealing with the boyfriend. Less than a year with him, I was introduced to alcohol and drugs. Not realizing I was tied to him mentally and emotionally, I too thought that once I moved that was it. I had no problem attempting to move on, but he did. Since he knew I would be transferred to work for the same company, it didn't take long for him to look up the store number and call me. Although I never turned down the conversations, I kept them short because I was at work.

Here is where many young ladies find themselves. Men will prey on your need to be needed. He amped up the calls once I turned eighteen, only three months after I graduated. Not only did he amp up the calls, he amped up the pressure. Pressure to do what? The pressure to leave home and go back to Orlando to live with him. Call after call he told me he loved me and missed me. Oh, how he needed me. This joker even fake cried on the phone. It didn't take me long to cave under the pressure. One night I went home after quitting my job and told my parents that I was going to live with him. How was I going to get there?

In the car he bought me. My mother cried and I know I broke my parent's heart. I left my little sister behind, which opened up a doorway for her to rebel in her own way, partially due to my absence. I didn't weigh out what I was going to do, nor did I think about the future.

Let me tell you, when I showed up at his place and saw the cavalier way he was behaving, like I hadn't just uprooted what little life I had, I was livid. I started an argument with him as soon as I put my bags down. All those phone calls disturbing me on my job, crying, pleading with me to come stay with him, only to find him sitting in the bed reading a newspaper! No special greeting or anything. Needless to say, the argument was to no avail because I didn't leave. He didn't value me, and I couldn't see it, because I didn't value myself.

This was just the beginning of the downward spiral of my life with him. Eventually it was more than just crack and cocaine being sold. I became a user of cocaine. It gave me a rush; it made the sex seem greater and it lowered my inhibitions. It also opened the door for experimentation in the bedroom.

Just because a person is raised with parents who do their best for their child, instill good values, and let them know that there are consequences to all their actions, does not mean that at the age of eighteen they'll mature overnight. People can argue back and forth about having knowledge of right and wrong, being moral or immoral and the such. All it will ever do, as it has always done, is lead to more arguments, never solutions. The mind is something else and if it is perverted at an early stage in life, it will have a negative effect on their thinking. Just know that if you have a wayward child, please do not give up on them. Continue to teach them the right way and pray that if they wander too far, they'll come right back.

We moved closer to my old job with the same company and I started working again. Although, nothing slowed down the nighttime activity. Clubs, drugs, sex, and now meeting females to have threesomes. My life was out of control and I thought I was in full control.

Eventually I found a different job as a ticket agent. I was still living my crazy life, sleeping at best two to three hours and still going to work. It doesn't take a genius to know that you can only keep going like this only for so long before you crash and burn.

I dove deeper into partying and became what some would call a functioning druggie. On my days off from work, I would binge on sex and cocaine all the way up to the day I'd return to work. Sometimes I was high while at work. At this point, we were physically abusive with each other. Mostly, he would choke me and I would try to fight back. To make matters worse, he came to pick me up from work and on the way to get something to eat, we were arrested during my lunch hour.

He told me to take all the drugs out of the console, put them in my clothes and like an idiot, I did. Did I leave? No, and this was not the first time. Up to this point I experienced abuse, lying, and cheating. He was married, as I found out later, but eventually divorced. While on the job, I was confronted by a lady who was not his wife. Between the two of them, they had six kids. She was trying to let me know. By now I was in so deep that even though I knew I needed to break free from him, I was willing to stay with and keep him. I stayed through the back and forth with the baby mama drama, court cases and abuse. In addition, I faced the heartbreaking choice of ending a pregnancy with an abortion, something I live with even today.

We moved again. We did this a few times while we were together. The abuse worsened and I always fought back. My mindset was I wasn't going to take it. I was giving him a dose of his own medicine.

Like any other domestic violence situation, the abuse escalated from threatening, grabbing and burning my things, to choking until I started seeing black. I had scratches and marks and if they asked, I always told people it was nothing. Anyone with half a brain knew different. Just like most domestic violence situations, the woman is an adult and people want to say something, but most think she'll just stay or leave and come back. Most people never step in and at least say "you need to leave." The woman's decision will be her decision but at least say something, don't stay silent. If something tragic happens, at least you tried. It doesn't make you feel any better if something happens to the abused partner and you sat idly by and let it happen.

While we were living in yet another new place, we were arrested again. The police were looking for him from an old warrant and because I didn't immediately let them in, they accused me of harboring a fugitive. While I wasn't charged with that crime, they did charge me with possession of the drugs that were found in the house.

Within the few years we were together, I saw more than enough police to last me a lifetime. There was so much that transpired during those years that it all won't fit into this chapter. In the end, by the grace of God, I was given five years of probation. I moved back with my family until I found my own place and after eight years of receiving calls from him at no matter which retail store I worked, he finally moved on with his life and left me alone.

Be assured that regardless of whatever dark past we lived, does not have to write our future. I know without a shadow of a doubt that I am not the spiritually depraved person I was then. Submitting my life to God, loving Him above all, and loving others as I love myself has brought the greatest change in me.

There is life afterwards and there is love waiting on the other side of all the wrong choices in life we made. That may sound cliché', but I promise, I am a living witness.

About the Author

Myesha Marie Miller was born and raised in Waukegan, Illinois. Her mother married her stepfather and during high school, the family moved to Orlando, Florida. The year of graduating high school, at the age of seventeen, her family moved to Orange Park, Florida. In 2013, she was ordained a minister of the gospel of Christ. In 2016, she received a bachelor's degree in Christian ministry from North Florida Theological Seminary.

Myesha is the founder of Breaking the Silence Seminars, which conducts yearly events to address challenging topics such as generational cycles of sin, dysfunctional relationships, personal insecurities and more. The seminar provides an environment for openly discussion and to provide answers and strategies for a better mindset and productive life. Myesha is the single mother of one son named Chance.

To book Myesha Marie Miller to speak at your seminar or event: E-mail her at generationsse@gmail.com or call (904) 377-7356.

Pastor Polly Sanders-Peterson

Getting Untied from the Past:
Overcoming the Feelings and Belief of Rejection

Holding on to past unresolved issues such as rejection, punishment, bitterness, hurt, wounds, shame, anger, fear, great disappointments, and unmet emotional needs, not only caused conflicts in my life and relationships but left me tied up in my soulish realm, mind, emotions, and will.

> ### 1 Thess. 5:23
>
> *²³ May God himself, the God of peace, sanctify you through and through. May your whole spirit, soul and body be kept blameless at the coming of our Lord Jesus Christ.*

God Wanted Me to Be Free

God wanted to untie me from my negative thinking, wounds, hurts, rejection, past lies, and deceptions so I would be free to live the bountiful life and future he has planned for me.

> **Psalm. 147:3**
> ³ *He heals the brokenhearted and binds up their wounds*. And
> **Isa. 61:1**
> *The Spirit of the Sovereign LORD is on me, because the LORD has anointed me to proclaim good news to the poor. He has sent me to bind up the broken hearted, to proclaim freedom for the captives and release from darkness for the prisoners*

My false belief systems caused me to live in a place with lack of hope and disappointments, discouragements, discontentment, depression, and finally in a place of despair, where I wanted to just give up and die!

> **John 10:10**
> ¹⁰ *The thief comes only to steal and kill and destroy; I have come that they may have life and have it to the full.*

God revealed to me that when I'm physically sick or injured, I see or feel signs in my body and must seek help. God also showed me signs when my soul was sick (mind, emotions, will). **(1 Thess. 5:23)**

I didn't recognize them as easily. Some of these signs included feelings of wanting to be loved and accepted, low self-esteem, rejection, insecurity, constantly falling back into the same bad relationships, and unresolved anger, bitterness, rebellion, and shame (self-hatred).

> ### *Psalm. 34: 17-19*
> *17 The righteous cry out, and the LORD hears them; he delivers them from all their troubles.*
> *18 The LORD is close to the brokenhearted and saves those who are crushed in spirit.*
>
> *19 The righteous person may have many troubles, but the LORD delivers him from them all;*

These led me to great inner issues with control, manipulation, works, anger, bitterness, rebellion, addictions, strongholds, and codependency. I felt that I would never measure up or be good enough (those are all lies of the enemy/Satan).

> ### Psalm. 34: 4-5
> 4 I sought the LORD, and he answered me; he delivered me from all my fears.
> 5 Those who look to him are radiant; their faces are never covered with shame.
> ### Exodus 14:14
> *14 The LORD will fight for you; you need only to be still."*

When God revealed this to me, it helped me realize why there were so many relationship issues, conflicts, and feelings of inferiority in my life, and why I could not overcome inner hurts, rejection, shame, guilt, and insecurity. It was no wonder I had little belief in myself and felt nothing would ever change for me. Lie! Wrong thinking! **(John 10:10)**

God began to reveal His unconditional love for me and drew me to His living Word. He gave me a hunger for Him, His truth and Word.

> **James 4:8**
>
> *⁸ Come near to God and he will come near to you. Wash your hands, you sinners, and purify your hearts, you double-minded.*
>
> **Eph. 2:22**
>
> *²² And in him you too are being built together to become a dwelling in which God lives by his Spirit.*
>
> **Deut. 6:5**
>
> *⁵ Love the LORD your God with all your heart and with all your soul and with all your strength.*
>
> **Jer. 29:13**
>
> *¹³ You will seek me and find me when you seek me with all your heart.*

How I Became Free

In **Luke 4:18**, My Father God delivered me and healed my broken heart/life.

> *¹⁸ "The Spirit of the Lord is on me, because he has anointed me to proclaim good news to the poor.*
> *He has sent me to proclaim freedom for the prisoners and recovery of sight for the blind, to set the oppressed free,*

Once I was willing to let the Rhema—the truth of God's Word—untie me from my negative past, there were four basic steps I needed to take to become FREE! (John 8:36)

1. I ACKNOWLEDGED that my soul was sick.

2. I QUIT BLAMING OTHERS and looked at what I could do to make Godly changes.

3. I SOUGHT GOD AND ASKED HIM to heal me in that area of my soul (emotions), will, and mind.

Jer. 17:14

14 Heal me, LORD, and I will be healed;
save me and I will be saved,
for you are the one I praise.

4. I ASKED GOD TO FORGIVE ME of all my sins of unrighteousness, like punishments, resentments, anger, bitterness, strongholds, pride, rebellion, and all known or unknown sins.

1 John 1:9

9 If we confess our sins, he is faithful and just and will forgive us our sins and purify us from all unrighteousness.

Psalm. 51: 10

10 Create in me a pure heart, O God,
and renew a steadfast spirit within me.

As I prayed with my heart and will and chose to apply God's love and word over my mind, will and emotions, healing has come from the inside out.

Exodus 15:26,

26 He said, "If you listen carefully to the LORD your God
and do what is right in his eyes, if you pay attention to
his commands and keep all his decrees, I will not bring
on you any of the diseases I brought on the Egyptians,
for I am the LORD, who heals you."

Psalm 30:2,

²LORD my God, I called to you for help, and you healed me.

Psalm 147:3

³He heals the brokenhearted and binds up their wounds.

What I Learned

Being tied up by past hurts, wounds, shame, rejection, and bitterness kept me from God's goodness, love, blessing, healing power, and divine purpose.

God's desire for my life and your life is for health, joy, peace, the fullness of healthy relationships, love, and power to move freely in our hearts and life!

If you are willing to allow Him to work in your heart, life, God will heal your soul, your broken heart and untie you from the past. You will find unceasing, unconditional love, total inner healing, acceptance, value, worth, forgiveness and divine purpose for your life "WITH HIM"!

About the Author

Pastor Polly is the founder and president of Covenant House of Love Ministries. She is also, a counselor, teacher, author, television and radio host, and a conference and seminar leader and speaker. Polly currently conducts women's support and counseling groups in the Colorado State Prisons System. She loves to mentor, teach and help emotionally wounded women become whole and come to know God's unconditional, unceasing love and build intimate relationship with God and the living Word of God. Polly is a published author of three books, *Love Search*, *Power of Perseverance* and *With Him*, all of which are available at Amazon.com.

To reach or find out more about Pastor Polly and her ministry work, to get help setting up inner healing groups in your area, or to start a prison ministry, visit www.CovenantHouseofLove.com or www.PollyandCo.com. You may also call (877) 744-2122 or (800) 584-0885.

Dr. Rochelle Gilbert

I AM – Intentionally, Authentically Me

The lens through which we visualize life's journey varies because of our perspective and vantage point on life. Our viewpoint is shaped by our perceptions, influenced by our environment, experiences, and beliefs. As women, too often we propel others, family, friends and colleagues, ahead and risk disregarding ourselves. This inattention to self becomes habit, through trying to save others, being everyone else's super-SHERO, and by merely failing to walk in God's calling for our own lives.

As little girls, we are taught how to care for ourselves and others. We are taught early in life to take care of family, help community, support the church, all while handling our own individual situations and issues. We project a sometimes unrealistic view of the ease of being all to everyone! Nurturers by nature, we often fall into the habit of "SHOE" wearing, if you will. Others call it wearing multiple hats; however, since I love shoes, we will go with SHOEs. Read on to discover why.

At home and in our family, we wear the various shoes of daughter, sister, niece, mother, fiancé, wife, and lover. In the world, the well-worn shoes of friend, colleague, co-worker, boss, manager, teacher, doctor, and many more. Even at church, we wear specific shoes, that of member, usher, musician, missionary, counselor, planner, announcer, choir member, preacher, usher, women's day chair, you name it. As women, we wear a lot of distinct shoes. The point is, there are shoes for each of our roles in life. Whether stilettos or pumps, tennis shoes or sneakers, peep-toe or kitten heels, sandals or flip flops, espadrilles or wedges, flats or Mary Janes, oxfords or loafers, mules or slingbacks, slippers and too many other types to name, they were designed for a special function. The selection depends on the exact occasion; nevertheless, and clearly, like all of these different pairs of shoes, women are frequently called to fill countless roles for everyone else in our lives. So much so, it becomes easy to allow ourselves to be pulled, sometimes yanked, in many directions while continuing to lose the battle for balance.

Because of this set standard for who we are, women often follow a pathway or journey that does not allow us to practice self-care. We are so inundated with satisfying the needs of everyone else that it becomes easy to fall prey to self-neglect. We forget to take a break to focus on our number one . . . Ourselves. Satisfied with being the caregiver, we start to settle for that pair of well-worn shoes, so much so that we Submit Her to Other Expectations (SHOE). The her I am referring to is YOU! It is me! It is the being inside of each of us who has forgotten who God called Her to be! Yes, He called us to be givers of love. He called us out to capture the true essence of life, leveling (balance), living, and leading. Yes, He called us to manifest the true essence of the our self-worth, yet He did not call us to burn ourselves out in the process.

If we fail to address self-actualization on our own, we will remain in a place of non-growth, fearing to step outside of the comfortable shoes that have become so familiar, whether subconsciously or consciously. We must learn self-value, meaning we must know who we are! We must heighten our self-esteem to become the person we want to be. We must know and appreciate our self-worth, and we must BELIEVE that we are who we say we are!

For over forty years I have fought for the privileges of everyone else, while sometimes selling myself short of personal victories. I have played investigative attorney, written letters, and challenged the debt collectors so I can help others. I have worn the shoes of support worker without the benefit of self-sufficiency. Do not get me wrong, it is lovely to back others up and come to the aid of the people you care about. While providing that support, be careful not to lose yourself in the interim.

Through self-inflicted stress, often I have allowed myself to be the impetus of my own deprivation and hindrance. My willingness to put the needs of helping a friend build a business ahead of developing my own, meant I came to the aid of others as I'd been encouraged to do. I have authored business plans and given away personal business secrets without compensation to ensure that success of a friend, two friends, three friends, and even my own family could be manifested. Sometimes it was because they had the capital and I did not venture out nor dare to step out on faith to secure financial backing. I had the business acumen yet lacked the determination to create my own personal brand. I had a business in name only, with a few clients, all the while supporting and ensuring everyone else's companies grew and their financial house was appropriately managed. I gave my time and energy to their projects using my expertise, skills, and knowledge base. Ultimately, wearing the familiar shoes of supporter, I forgot about ME and my needs completely!

I put on the shoes of friendship, the shoes of family, but I left off the shoes of FAITH. I have been the stimulus of discomfort because of my heartfelt inclination to help others build their empires, while I sat on the sidelines to watch their winning touchdowns. Cheering and supporting others came at the cost of the work I put it, the coaching I did, all without recognition that I was even on their team. Too often, I have been the provocation of deficiency because of my drive to work to grow someone else's relationship, while my relationships suffered. I have worn the shoes of counselor, confidante, and coach. I loved it, I LOVE it, and at the same time, it has brought me to the point of "What About ME?" I give and I gave. All of this, until one day, I made a conscious decision of, "No More!" I had to say YES to ME!

Like yours, my story is one where doing good for others somehow created self-inflicted doubt, procrastination and self-neglect. I doubted what I could do for me because I was so busy doing well for everyone else. I procrastinated on taking care of the one person all these other people depended on. I neglected myself to the degree that I gained weight; not mere physical pounds but the burden of other people's problems, their needs, and their dreams. So much weight that the scale was near tipping over.

As accomplished as I was, I realized that if I didn't take my life back, I was going to lose it for real. I had to reestablish my expectations for my life and define my limits and boundaries. Digging deeper into my Bible day after day, scripture slapped me in my face.

Hebrews 12:1 "*Wherefore seeing we also are compassed about with so great a cloud of witnesses, let us lay aside every weight and the sin which doth so easily beset us, and let us run with patience the race that is set before us.*" I had to remove any burden that was keeping me from Christ-likeness or holding me from answering His call for ME, not for others, but for me! This scripture showed me perseverance, growth and maturity; also that no matter what I may face, God's faithfulness would reign for me. I was charged by this scripture to strive to fulfill the plans God has for me; HIS plan, not mine!

God has set before us a foot race that we can genuinely win if we rely on Him as our Coach. We have to take self out of it and listen to His direction. We do this by avoiding obstacles such as the needs of the world and instead devote ourselves to seeking God's voice for guidance. We have to learn not to destroy our own self-worth which begins when we assign value to things outside of ourselves and outside of Him. We cannot accept the responsibility to care for and maintain things that have more value than we do. To win this race, we must support and nurture that inner Woman, the one who fortifies herself and does not tear herself down to build others up.

Likewise, I was reminded of my favorite scripture, Luke 1:45 which reads, *"And blessed is she that believed: for there shall be a performance of those things which were told her from the Lord."* I had to recognize my worth and take my power back. I had to acknowledge that it was not anyone's fault but mine that I did not could not or have not moved beyond my coulda woulda shouldas to my I AM!!! I had to realize that no one was holding me back, except me, and I have the power to draft a new story as I am the author of that story. I made the decision to focus on the world and not me, thus it is my job to redirect and refocus that energy.

Faith is represented in this scripture as it is the foundation of receiving the fulfillment of God's promises to us. God promised you that new house, it's yours! God promised you that family; it's yours! God promised you that business; it's yours! Whatever He has spoken, he shall perform based merely on the authority of WHO HE IS!!! It is the power of God, the one who is able to do all things; the faithfulness of God, the one who will never fail us or let us down; the veracity of God, the one who is authentic and cannot lie; and the experiences of the believer who has never been failed by God, that venerates us as women to BE our own God-Ordained selves.

You see, all of the shoes we wear can break us down as women if we do not learn to define who we are, what we want, and what we need to do to change environments and characterize our worth! I had to take ME back, reimagine who I AM as a woman. I had to create a space to fall in love with ME again and LOVE me to point or a new HERizon! The Lord had to speak to me and let me know that there is more to Me than what others see, more to me that just wearing the SHOES they had picked out for me, more to me than living for my next purchased pair . . . You see, every time I get settled in complacency, God pokes me and makes me get up. These shoes are only shoes of discomfort, shoes where size limitations are challenged, but there is fitting space, a season where God is ready to take the limits off!!! No pair is too small; no pair is too big. They come in every color and style — a place where the shoes are only made for you. No one else can fit them. GOD is demanding more of YOU, of ME!!!! He wants us to focus on Him so that we can align our lives to self-discovery. If you have lived my story, be like me as I am forgetting those things behind me . . . *I am reaching for those things before me . . . I am pressing forward towards the MARK of a HIGHER Calling (Philippians 3:14)!!!* Hallelujah!!! #IAM. What about you?

There is a saying that if you place a shark in a fish tank, it will only grow to the size of the tank; it never outgrows its environment. However, if you put that shark in the ocean, it will grow eight to ten feet easily. If we as women step into the vast oceans of God's journey for our lives, we will rise to our full purpose, potential, and position as promised. Take time out for yourself today. Buy that dress, read that book, better yet, write that book for yourself. Create space to **Seek Him**

Over **E**verything! That is your SHOE pledge. It's the SHOE to wear to gain back your **IAM** mentality. To be Intentionally Authentically ME!

About the Author

Dr. Rochelle Gilbert is a Change Agent, Personal Development and Executive Life Coach, and Chief Energy Officer. She is the owner of THERO LLC, a professional services firm and of Dr. RO and Associates, a 501(c)3 that offers training, consulting, coaching, teaching, and speaking to individuals, corporations, and organizations in the public, private, and non-profit areas.

As the Founder of "I AM - Intentionally Authentically ME," Dr. Rochelle is passionate about helping others to achieve their "NEXT" in Life through Balance and Impact! Her goal is to move people from what others think and feel about them to the I AM principle, appreciating and embracing all that GOD has created them to be and MORE!

Contact Dr. Rochelle directly at dr.rochelle.gilbert@outlook.com, visit her website at www.rochellegilbert.com or call her directly at (318) 278-9876. Also, be sure to connect with her on Facebook @THEDRRO.

Roxanne Smith

Gifted, Frustrated and Broken

The alarm clock goes off, I hit the snooze button and wish I didn't have to get up. As I lay in bed, I think, "Can I just lay here in the dark, alone, where no one can call my name and expect me to have some powerful word or answer? I don't want to deal with the pressure. I just want to lay here and forget about this thing everyone calls a gift." Have you ever had a morning like this? If so, keep reading, this chapter is for you.

Like you, I've had too many of these days to count. But it wasn't always like this for me. There was a time when I woke up excited about life and ready to go full force, demolishing any obstacle in my way. When you consider the fact that I was born to parents who were prophets and children's ministers, you may be able to see where this is going. My parents were gifted in activating children in the prophetic and teaching them the Word of God, which was rare back in the 80s.

At the age of four, I was standing on a crate, leading children in worship with my older sister, while my father and older brother played the guitar. My mother did the hand motions to the songs and my middle brother played the drums. I stood on that same crate to go behind the puppet stage and help put on shows for the kids to teach them about Jesus. I ate it up! The creativity and freedom that I felt was electrifying. I was in the zone! I couldn't get enough of learning and growing in the things of God, as well as helping others do the same. My parents recognized my passion and began to train me in the way I should go. By the time I was twelve, I had delivered my first sermon and was holding Bible studies in the lunchroom at school. I was on fire and everyone knew it.

People told my parents how much they enjoyed my ministry and admired my relationship with God. They would go on and on about how gifted I was. At that time, I didn't think it was such a big deal. I just knew that I loved God. I loved to feel His presence overtake me as I read the Bible and sang worship songs. I loved praying for people, giving them a prophetic word and watching them be healed from sickness right before my eyes. These were some of the best moments of my life. Where others saw the gift, I just saw the love between a girl and the 'Gift Giver.' Nothing else mattered. But little did I know that would soon change.

In high school, my love for God was tested as I was often made fun of for my acne scarred face, thick framed glasses and bringing my Bible to school. The adults that once before sang my gifts' praises never told me about the persecution I'd experience. I was not prepared for the separation that was beginning to take place. Though I loved to study God's Word, I had no one my age to share revelation with, not even the kids at church. I finally got so tired of trying to share with my peers, that I began to spend a lot of time alone in my room. There, I would write poems and songs in tear-stained journals, trying to ease the pain of being different. I remember praying and asking God, "Why me? Why did you give me all of this and make me to be alone?"

My parents would tell me that I had to protect my anointing and that it would cost me something. But who wants to hear that as a kid? Who really wants to hear that at any age? Telling me that my gifts would cost me something was like saying, "I brought you the present you wanted but you have to pay me for it." It was a concept I couldn't seem to understand. Why would God give me something at the time of birth and then want me to pay Him for it? What was I supposed to give Him? This sent me on a wild goose chase trying to find the right payment for the Gift Giver. Oh, the things I've tried to pay with. Some of which never needed to be sacrificed in the first place.

I began to think that in order to properly pay for this gift I needed to be perfect. Perfection had to be the best form of payment, I thought. And that's where the frustration began. No matter how hard I tried, I just couldn't be perfect. I tried reading my Bible and praying more. I tried to be the nicest, sweetest girl you'd ever met. This led me down a path of people pleasing that literally caused me to lose my mind as an adult, but we'll get into that later.

Though the Word never said that I had to be perfect, it seemed like everyone around me felt that way. So, for me not to make the wrong move and lose the anointing, I drew further and further away from others to protect myself. Not only did I pull further away from my peers, I pulled further away from my family. I had to. If I didn't, they would find out my secret. I really wasn't perfect. I had done something wrong. I allowed the worse sin to creep in and it was all my fault, I thought. I couldn't tell anyone. They'd blame me and things wouldn't be the same again.

As a minister, I wasn't supposed to have been touched. I was supposed to be pure and holy, not damaged and dirty. Just like that, I held it all in and suffered in silence. Resentment slowly made its way on the scene. I did my best to cover it up with isolation. The more I was alone, the more frustrated I became. No one ever knew anything was wrong because they thought my room was where I would spend time with God, but it became my house of depression, fear and rejection. My room was where I tried to hide from the truth. There was so much more going on than I could ever admit. Nothing I did seemed to take away the pain. I believe this is where the spirit of suicide found an open door. It came in and I was completely unaware until I had a full encounter with the unwelcome visitor.

The battle raged on and I kept preaching, teaching, and giving to others as if nothing was wrong. I remember one of my classmates asked me to pray for them because they wanted to commit suicide. I prayed for them at school and they said they felt better, but after the prayer, I felt worse. I was dealing with the spirit of suicide myself so praying for my peer only increased my own warfare. The problem was I didn't have the proper weapons to fight. I had prayed for my classmate without being covered myself or receiving the natural care I needed. That spirit just intensified within me. When I got home, I grabbed a knife and sat on the pool deck ready to take my own life. I was tired of everyone else getting better when I prayed for them, while I still was hurting when I prayed for myself. This gift people said I had felt more like a curse and I was over it!

As I put the knife to my wrist a bright light stood before me and I dropped the knife. All I remember after that is waking up from "a nap" on the deck, to the sound of my mother calling me. I looked around and the knife was gone. The walk to my room that day was so long. When I arrived at my house of depression, I closed the door, laid in the fetal position and cried like a baby. I heard a voice say, "It's not your time. I have much for you to do. I love you." For fear of not being seen the same in the eyes of others, I never shared this experience. I didn't want them to be disappointed with me. I knew that suicide was a sin and I was more ashamed now than ever. There I was at 14 years old, sexually abused, broken, frustrated, and gifted.

Twenty years later the same problem existed. Except now, not only did I have unresolved little girl issues, I had woman issues. You know the issues that keep you from being able to stand in a room full of women and feel comfortable. Those issues that have you looking at your body and feeling less than. The issues that make you question if you're really a good wife and mother. I was the perfect example of leading while bleeding. My gifts had opened many doors for me but there were many that were closed because of my age and gender. Other male ministers were intimidated by my creativity and boldness. I was good enough to help them build the ministry but not man enough to lead it. No matter how many meetings I went to, Bible studies I led, and God-given ideas that they used, they only saw me as a young gifted girl.

Despite what people may say, being a powerful woman in the church is still not fully accepted by men. Mix that with being in your twenties and you become a threat. I began to feel defeated in the arena I once soared in. It was as if every time I began to soar my wings would get clipped and I'd have go through the long process of growing them out again. Whenever man said, "The Lord told me to give this to you," it never happened. Over and over again I was told this is yours, but I never received it and I couldn't understand why. I had given so much. I missed my kids' events, drug them all over the church, skipped cooking dinners and came home late at night, thinking if I just did whatever people needed me to do then I could prove that I was good enough to have what they claimed God said was mine.

I tried my best to do whatever they asked, so they could be pleased with me. I needed the approval of others in order to survive. It was my drug and I was its user. The people pleasing preacher junkie. I couldn't function without it. I was so busy trying to please people that I forgot about pleasing God. I found myself too often paying the cost with my family as well as my own peace. My marriage suffered. My children only knew mommy inside the four walls. I didn't even know who I was or what I wanted anymore. It was like I was going through the motions. Ministry turned into something that I no longer loved and once again I despised the gift. Proverbs 18:16 says, "A man's gift makes room for him and brings him before great men." I just wanted to know what room my gift was making for me. Every room that I thought was mine became a prison.

It wasn't until 2016 that I realized I was stuck in a vicious cycle. Though I had ministered to hundreds of people, preached on many platforms, led folks to Jesus and even taught children how to prophesy and walk in their gifts, I was yet a frustrated and broken little girl. My frustration began to manifest all the time in my home, ministry and on the job. I had a short fuse and was snapping at everyone. Gone was the positive, up-beat façade I had hidden behind all those years. This woman right here was flat out angry. One evening I got so upset over something minor and I totally lost it. My body became boiling hot. I started to hear all these voices in my head and no matter what I did, I could not move my body. The voices continued to grow louder and louder. I knew if I didn't do something I was going to be locked up in the psychiatric ward or worse, end up dead.

A few minutes later, I mustered up enough strength to scream, "Jesus!" Immediately the voices ceased. The silence was deafening, and the dark room seemed to close in on me. As I regained control of my limbs, my mind was blank. What just happened? I completely lost control of myself and entered a rage that I never felt before. Then all the memories I tried so hard to suppress came flooding into my mind. I knew in that moment something in my life needed to change. I needed to change. No longer could I ignore the issues of my heart. No more could I hold onto the secrets of my past. No more could I continue to bulldoze through life. It was obvious that this tough machine called Roxane was seriously broken.

You might be saying there had to be signs way before this. You're right there were many. I stated a few in the beginning of this chapter. However, when you have learned religious behaviors as I have, you don't ever really deal with the root of a thing. All my life I've seen believers smile and say, "I'm blessed," as if their life is all good. When in all actuality they're hurting, and things are not so good. "Where there is no guidance, a people fall, but in an abundance of counselors there is safety." Proverbs 11:14 (ESV). The fact of the matter is, everyone wants to guide the gift but it's much harder to find an abundance of true counselors who provide safety. For many of us, if we had felt safe our lives would have been much different.

I am grateful that when I had my mental breakdown God sent me an abundance of counselors. One of which told me that I needed to go to counseling. I was not open this idea at first. In the black community it's taboo. We're not encouraged to seek help, instead we're told to be strong and keep it moving. But after months tossing the idea around, I finally booked my first appointment. I remember walking in the office for the first time. I wanted to turn around and run out but Prov. 11:14 kept me in my seat. As I began to share my life story, I could feel a

weight lifting. I was getting free from the lifelong bondage that had me bound.

The search is finally over! I discovered the cost that must be paid, and it's found in Matthew 26. Jesus went to the Garden of Gethsemane to pray and He asked the Lord to take the cup from Him. He knew the time had come to die. He also knew that for the promises of God to be fulfilled to man, He had to obey. I don't believe that Jesus was afraid to die. I believe because He was a man, His flesh didn't want to allow Him to die. In His choice to die, He was boldly telling the enemy, "I trust my Father and because He loves me, I will obey Him."

There's a big difference in what the spirit wants and what the flesh wants. Samuel said it best, "to obey is better than to sacrifice." Jesus knew that the real test was and has always been His obedience, not His sacrifice. Religion has taught us to pay the price, but the price was paid when Jesus died on the cross. We don't need to try to be perfect, we have grace. We don't have to seek to please people by holding secrets, being the yes man, or putting our families on the back burner. All God really wants is our obedience. Then you will see Him transform your brokenness into beauty, turn your frustration into fruition, and use your gifts for His glory.

About the Author

Roxane Smith is an inspirational speaker and business creative. Her passion is to help others recognize their gifts and provide the them with the tools needed to live their dreams and fulfill their purpose.

Roxane has preached the Word of God to adults and children and operating in the prophetic for more than two decades. She began preaching at the age of twelve and became a licensed minister at twenty-one. She has played a significant role in the development of various children's ministries, five-fold ministry teams, school of the prophets, prophetic prayer groups, and worship teams.

She resides in Cincinnati, Ohio, with her husband of ten years, Charles Smith Jr. and their six children. You can contact Roxane by email at theroxanesmith@gmail.com or by telephone at (513) 400-4621.

Ryan C. Greene

Re-Ignite Your Fire Within

Hold your hand on your belly. Do you feel that? Press harder. No? Nothing? Do you remember when there used to be a fire there? When a burning desire inside of you that drove your every action once resided in the depth of your belly? Remember that feeling? All that's left now is the smoldering ruins of what used to be your purpose, passion and dreams. The raging inferno that once fueled your life was left to become but a dim flicker and you've settled for a life of "good enough." What happened? Where did your fire go? Why did you let it die? More importantly, how do you re-ignite it?

We've all been there at some point in our lives. Anyone who lives a life of purpose and has ever chased a dream has at some point faced seasons of doubt, discomfort and darkness. Wanting to give up is a very real challenge. Pushing through times of lack and little motivation isn't a foreign concept to those who are striving to achieve the highest calling on their lives. It's just a fact of life that at some point, everyone's fire fades along the journey. The difference in those who end up living a mediocre mundane life and those who live a fantastically fulfilled life is how they push through those periods and re-ignite their fire within.

So, what happens when your fire goes out? How do you light the flames again? Successful people aren't successful because they always got it right along the way. They're not successful because they never faced challenges and quit. Successful people are successful because even in their darkest hour, when their destiny seemed to be most out of reach, they buckled down and found a way to stay the course and continue toward their ultimate goal. Quitting is not that unnatural and wanting to give up is not that foreign a concept when you are pursuing something great. The key factor, however, separating those who succeed and those who fail is the innate desire to start back up after you have quit.

In my new book *Becoming A Passionpreneur*, I share many lessons on how to build passion-driven revenue streams and how to make a living doing what you love. All of it starts with setting goals. Goal setting is one of the cornerstones of any success blueprint. Every professional has been through some level of goal setting training. Who hasn't been taught how to set S.M.A.R.T. goals a hundred times in their career? It's become one of those concepts that we all know is critical, yet we seem to also take for granted.

Think about the last big goals you set. Did you achieve those goals, or did you quit? Why do so many of us give up on our goals that once meant so much to us when we were crafting them? If we're setting S.M.A.R.T. goals, you know, specific, measurable, action-oriented, realistic, time-sensitive goals, then why do so many of us continue to fall short on achieving them? More importantly, why do so many of us not even care when we do?

That's the quandary I searched to solve when I created S.T.U.P.I.D. Goals. Just like S.MA.R.T. goals, S.T.U.P.I.D. is an acronym. Each letter stands for an important element necessary for setting goals that will be impossible for you to quit. S.T.U.P.I.D goals fill in the missing elements of effective goal setting and help you plan for obstacles before you begin. When you know what to expect and how to better deal with the roadblocks you'll inevitably face along the way, you will have far greater success in achieving your goals.

So, what are S.T.U.P.I.D Goals? Let's get to it!

SACRIFICE: *What are you willing to give up to achieve your goal?*

Knowing what you are willing to give up before you get started is the most critical part of setting goals you won't quit on before completing. Far too often, leaders set great goals on paper without ever contemplating the true price it will take to achieve it. You need to know going in just how much time, money, family time, travel, late nights, and more, it will take to achieve your goal. Are you willing to miss the kid's recitals and date night with your spouse in order to achieve your goal? How much money are you willing to sink into your idea before you decide enough is enough? You don't want to wait until you're deep into your journey to realize the road is too rough for you to tread. Before you embark upon your goals, take an honest inventory of all the necessary sacrifices your goal requires and decide if you're willing to give up those things in order to achieve them.

TEAM: *Who is going to help you achieve your goal?*

John C. Maxwell said, "No great accomplishment was ever achieved by one person alone." Any goal worth achieving is going to require a team who helps you achieve it. Don't wait until your back is against the wall to find help. Expect upfront to need other people to help you be great. People are your number one resource in business and leadership. The weak leader says, "If it's going to get done right, I have to do it myself." The stronger leader asks, "Who do I know who can do this task better than me?"

UPLIFTING: *Where is your goal taking you that's better than now?*

What good is a goal if it doesn't take you to a higher level in some area of your life? The whole purpose of setting goals is because there's something out there that's better than what you have, somewhere out there that's better than where you are, someone out there who's better than who you are. The pitfall most goal setting exercises fall into is they never force you to explicitly articulate and illustrate what that thing is. If there's some level you're trying to achieve, you need to as vividly and explicitly as possible articulate that when setting your goals. Being able to look at that new level and see it before you reach it, will motivate you in ways unimaginable during the tough times. It's that aspiration that will drive you when you want to quit. If you don't have that written out, you'll find yourself quitting every time the road gets rough.

PLAN: *How do you plan to achieve your goal?*

"He who fails to plan, plans to fail." That quote is attributed to Winston Churchill with a little ghostwriting from Benjamin Franklin. "Poor execution will kill even the greatest of ideas". That quote is attribute to ME. (Did you peep that double entendre?) Your goal is only as strong as your plan to achieve it. Here's why your team is so vital. You won't have all the answers. If you think you do have all the answers, I can assure you they're not all the best answers. Collaboration trumps isolation all day. Don't confuse your "plan" with your "strategy" or your "tools". Your PLAN is the detailed day-by-day measurable activities you will use to reach your goal. Your strategy is the means by which you will accomplish your plan. Your tools are the specific things you use to implement your strategy. So, your plan may be to reach 1,000 new prospects in the next six months. Your strategy may be to do a daily online social media blitz. Your tools would then be Facebook, Twitter, and Instagram. Too often I see people confuse their tools with their plan. Facebook is not a plan, it's a tool.

INSPIRED: *Why are you going after your goal?*

Inspired is not to be confused with uplifting. When making sure your goal is uplifting, it is more about WHERE you want to go. When ensuring that your goals are inspired, it is about understanding WHY you want to go there. If your *why* is big enough, the *how* will figure itself out. Every goal you set must have a strong level of inspiration behind it or else why would you even pursue it? When determining your inspiration for your goals, I'd challenge you to do a few things. First, use something you can be proud of and enjoy as your inspiration. Secondly, make it about someone other than yourself. It's much easier to quit on yourself than it is to quit on someone who's counting on you. Maybe it's your kids, maybe your spouse or parents, maybe it's your team, or maybe it's total strangers who will benefit from your achievement. Finally, find inspiration that will make you cry if you quit. If the thought of quitting on your goal doesn't bring real tears to your eyes, then your why isn't big enough and your goal isn't as inspired as it could be.

DEADLINE: *When do you plan to achieve your goal?*

We've covered the Who, What, Where, How, and Why and all that's left is the When. Every goal needs to have a deadline attached. A goal without a deadline is simply a dream. You have to set a date and push for it. A 90-Day Blitz. A 24-Hour Marathon. Lose 15 pounds in 30 days. It doesn't matter the goal, if there's no deadline attached, it's a pointless venture. There's something about knowing in your mind that something has to get done by a certain date. Pareto's 80/20 Rule speaks to the idea that 80% of any task gets done in the last 20% of the time. So, if that's true, which I believe it is, then it's important to set that deadline so that your 80% kicks in. Think about how much more powerful "my goal is to lose 15 pounds in the next 30 days." sounds over "my goal is to lose 15 pounds." See the difference? Martin Luther King, Jr. talked about "the fierce urgency of now". When accomplishing goals, a deadline builds in an automatic fierce urgency which pushes us to action.

Setting goals is critical to your success, but your success is measured by actually achieving the goals you set. When you begin setting S.T.U.P.I.D. goals, it will become impossible to quit on your goals because you've now set goals based on what truly matters to you and moves you. It's my goal to see more people set goals that work for them so they can achieve the success they desire. That being said, I don't want you to simply have this information. I want you to read it and apply it to your life right away. **You can get a FREE copy of my audio download "Setting S.T.U.P.I.D. Goals" by texting the word GOALS to (614) 333-0338.** You will receive an audio download as well as a "Setting S.T.U.P.I.D. Goals" Worksheet for you to begin setting your goals today.

Your goals are worth it! You are worth it! You ARE a woman of worth!

About the Author

Whether via a stage in front of thousands, over the radio and television airwaves, or through one of his many books, "The Passionpreneur" Ryan C. Greene is the authority on living your best life and making a living doing what you love by building passion-driven revenue streams. Since 2005, Ryan has impacted crowds from colleges to corporations, from laymen to leaders, and empowered them with the vision and belief to take ownership of their passion and turn their dreams into revenue machines! Having shared stages with speaking greats like Willie Jolley, Delatorro McNeal II, and George Fraser, Ryan is quickly becoming one of the nation's most sought-after trainers on leadership, personal and professional development, content development, and sales writing.

Ryan C. Greene is an entrepreneur, certified author coach, bestselling author, and professional speaker. He is the founder of GreeneHouse Media LLC, a media company whose goal is to provide "Media With A Purpose" via radio, television, film, and books. Ryan is the author of six books, the host of *The Passionpreneurs Podcast* and founder of Six-Figure Author Mastery. He specializes in teaching authors and speakers how to monetize their content, automate their business and boost their revenue.

For more information or to book Ryan C. Greene to speak for your organization or to present at your next event, please visit www.RyanCGreene.com.

Serita Love

Adversity

Let me tell you about my shoes. They are soooo uncomfortable, but I ALWAYS rock them with a smile. No one would ever expect that I have some of the secrets that I hold within these shoes. I didn't even expect to withhold some of them myself, but now I understand why. Sometimes, you must do whatever you have to do to make your dreams come true! When you haven't been delivered a silver spoon, life is a little more difficult. You become more creative when you have an intense desire to succeed. It will be a very rare occasion that someone comes to save you, so do not count on being saved. So many people are out here for themselves, not realizing how much more rewarding life would be if they served others. When you fully appreciate this, you will immediately understand why you should never bank on someone to do what you aren't willing to do for yourself. I know, I know. Life isn't fair and you have all these things you have to do that deter you from going after what's yours! Honestly, I don't wanna hear it. We have all been through stuff. We will all go through things and very few of us come out on top. I believe that with everything inside of me that you are one of those few. Walk with me, as I explain what I mean.

Upbringing

I come from a lower-class environment, where it was (and still is) normal to regularly interact with drug dealers, addicts, alcoholics, pedophiles, criminals and people who are satisfied with just getting by. Growing up, I had a feeling that there had to be more to life than what I saw. Then, I turned nine and my mother died. Losing my mother at the precious age of nine was a terrible experience. That loss left me with a feeling that I will never be able to fully describe. I cannot lie. Moving to new homes and schools, making new friends, and adapting to new environments, was hard! Shortly after my mother's death, I also started my period at the age of nine. To top it off, I had forty percent of frontal hair loss that I was teased about for a very long time. Kids accused me of having AIDS, cancer or leukemia. I believe I got a tetanus infection from my neighbor's dog. Fortunately for me, eventually my hair grew back. However, it took quite some time for the pain of the teasing to go away.

My upbringing was rather unique. I lived with five different relatives over the course of ten years, transferred to seven different schools (four of which I attended in the eighth grade), while remaining motivated to get ahead in life. Many times, things got hectic, but I was never sidetracked and I never allowed many to know what was going on in my absurd little world. I became known for smiling all the time and being involved in everything at school, especially if it involved leading the way. Back then, I was a *Success Junkie* but I didn't have a name for it at the time. My peers agreed.

My mother instilled something in me that would stick with me through every waking moment of my life. In her eyes, I was her little star. She said it was no accident I was born on the 4th of July, and that I was created to do something big. I never knew what that really meant, but I knew that I would someday find out. I took that to heart and always acted like I was somebody as I matured. I never cared about what people thought about how I felt about myself. In fact, when I started attending a new high school, I wore a gold star on my right eye every day. People probably thought I was a little wired, but it didn't bother me. Eventually, as life went on, I made it my business to make other people feel good, *through my word*s. Later, it was through my actions. I've always wanted to help people feel good about themselves, so it does not surprise me that I do what I do for a living: help people achieve their goals on their terms.

Oddly enough, I have made so many mistakes and I continue to make them as I grow. I have failed financially, got pregnant at nineteen, and failed (and still fail) at attempting to create relationship balance amongst loved ones. I have failed and failed and failed. In college, I was an *average* student at best, because I was easily distracted and didn't know how to balance personal struggles with things I had to tackle head on. My professors knew I could improve, and they admired my creativity. Being creative or a woman of many ideas is probably one of my most prized possessions. I work on enhancing my level of creativity, so I can strategically use that skillset to help people change their lives. We all have the one gift, or thing that everyone compliments us on. That gift is what you should be fine tuning in order to change your life. That gift may make you rich or allow you to create a life you never imagined was possible for you.

In life, adversity is inevitable. We have storms, combats, scarcity, violence and so many things going on in the world. Look at our personal lives. Many of us must deal with tragedies, confrontations, losses and deaths. The struggle of it all is virtually unbearable if we choose to focus exclusively on the negativity surrounding it. Most of these bad things that occur are beyond our control. What we do have control over, is how we deal with the negative circumstances. How we deal is all determined by how we think, and the way we think must be positive. When we are positive, more positive things happen and we become more confident to press fast forward on life. I have learned that when you are more positive during challenging times, the true qualities of who you are—your strength, courage and perseverance— arises from deep inside of you. With adversity comes wisdom and growth. It is your job to build up the courage, faith and resilience to press on. I'd like to share a few things with you, in hopes that they resonate with you in a great way. I like to believe they should be your adversity survival tips for success.

So, buckle up, and enjoy this ride!

Every single day will present a new mystery, a new discovery, a new situation and a new circumstance. Expect that, but do not expect to give up or give in. I always say that you must *grow through what you go through*. If you are reading this sentence right now, I take it that you take YOU very seriously. I also would like to assume that you understand you are a very rare breed. Most people you have grown up around do not think like you. On the flip side, you aspire to be around a more inspiring, like-minded group of peers. You are different, and that is okay. There are more people like you, waiting to meet you, to win with you. So, do not fret about being around people who don't understand your eagerness for ambition and success. You have work to do. This moment is only temporary, and your rewards await you.

Every day should present a new opportunity for you to be better than you were the day before. You must set yourself up for intentional progress and achievement. This will change your entire life, forever! When I was younger, I always knew I would grow up and see the world. I have been adamant about that for a very long time, and now I am acting to do exactly what I said I would do. I know you have big dreams, and you may have accomplished some of them. If not, let's just call this a bit of a cheat sheet for you to figure out how to make it happen!

When you refresh, reload and regroup, your personal confidence will be solidified. You will gain more strength to press on. You will believe you can achieve anything! I know this, because I have been there.

Your current situation is not your final destination.

If you understand this as soon as possible, you will fully understand what you can accomplish almost immediately in your life. You have to awaken your spirit to upgrade yourself to another level.

I hear people give every excuse in the wind about why they cannot step into the life they deserve. These people are stuck worrying about everyone else. Trying to be liked and accepted so badly that they forget who they are, or they never make time to find out. If you focus on the wrong things, you will never make time to succeed at the right things. You know you deserve better, but some people do not.

In order to jump over, climb under, and go through your current circumstance, you must change your mind. You have to change your mind about what you care about. You have to be okay with the person you know you are keeping yourself away from. How can one be afraid of a better version of themselves? There is a long list of reasons that are the answers to that question.

Are you ever afraid to open a gift that someone gives you? I'd like to assume that you probably are not. So, why would you be afraid of the gift God gave you? It was given to you for you to share. Your gift is to be of service and heal others. As you heal them, you heal yourself. This is the side effect to living in your purpose. You have to stop being too afraid, and just do what your heart tells you to.

To overcome adversity so you can truly head toward living the life only YOU can dream of, I have come up with several ways to overcome adversity. This is to put on some new shoes for your legacy from your lessons, to create the lifestyle you know you deserve.

Your success is within reach. You just have to believe if you work smart enough to achieve a realistic goal, you can bring it to fruition. In order to grow there are signs, resources, and people all around you to make use of and learn from. There are no "Do not enter" signs. Only your fears hold you back and make you feel inadequate. Sometimes we limit ourselves in ways that practically disable us from getting anywhere. It is really unfortunate that many people don't succeed because they count themselves out before they even place themselves in a position to be excellent or strive towards greatness.

To believe that you are capable when you don't know the first step to take, is empowering. Many of us start out not knowing where to begin, but that doesn't mean we lose the hunger to feed our minds with the proper nourishment to gain clarity and knowledge. When we were babies, many of us were very ambitious! Most of us strived to crawl or walk. Some of us skipped crawling, pulled ourselves up and began walking. Ambition varies from person to person, but almost all of us start off virtually fearless... to an extent. It is the life experiences of failure that discourages us from striving to get back up to try again. Many lack the willpower and many do not have enough willpower. You must have it set in your mind that no matter what, you will do whatever it takes to bounce back when you are pushed down. You cannot accomplish what you do not believe in, because you won't put your best foot forward. You cannot accomplish something when you have already claimed defeat. As easy as it is to give up, it isn't as rewarding.

No, everyone isn't going to be successful, but YOU are different. YOU are eager to become motivated to conquer fears and take off in a way that is most beneficial to you for the long haul. YOU aren't the type to stick to the basics. YOU want more, and you are willing to pay the price for excellence, and I don't blame you. If YOU are willing to go out there and get it, then you deserve to have it. No one deserves it more than a hard worker who is willing to fail in order to succeed. Why, you ask? Because achievement is beautiful!

You are not what you have been through. Many times, people accept their circumstance as their reality or truth. You do not have to be like them. They may not understand how much of a say they really have in their lives. But you are different. Even with all the hoops and hurdles that life sends you through, you will always be aware of what you can overcome when you set your mind up to do so. It's an amazing process, but every single time you take a step further, you will become stronger, smarter and wiser! It will become more challenging and every challenge will be welcomed. You really must be serious about how bad your desire is to become and remain triumphant. When you expect things to get hectic, you will be prepared for virtually anything that may come your way. That's the best part! Knowing that you have conditioned yourself to be great, will always be inspiration when you need your strength the most!

My life has been full of endless miracles, and unexpected events that have absolutely blown my mind—in good ways and bad. Sometimes, I feel undeserving of all the things that has been granted to me, because I have been extremely blessed beyond measure. Sometimes, I feel like this has happened to me so that I can focus on fulfilling my purpose. I've always wanted to become successful someday, but I knew the only way that I would be content about doing so, would be by helping others to succeed as well. It's difficult to be around consistent negativity and expect positivity. You literally must be crazy to have the strength to believe there has to be more out there in the world. Especially when all you hear for a long time is that where you are is where you will remain. When you think differently, your life changes.

The people around you change. Everything changes. That's the best thing about life. Even when things can affect you in the worse way possible, most times we almost always have a way to overcome life's worse case scenarios. Some of us have been conditioned to be negative because all we have been exposed to were negative people and negative experiences, which resulted into negative outlooks on life. No, everyday isn't going to be lily pads and daffodils, but life can be much greater when your mind is sound. When you are at peace with simplicity and constantly working on yourself is when the game changes. What you need is what you will attract, because you are commanding its undivided attention. So, attract good energy, good vibes, good circumstances by thinking that somehow, someway, it is already yours to have in your possession.

Conclusion

Adversity. You must understand that none of us are immune to it. It will happen and you will have to respond. The way you respond, however, will affect you all the days of your life. Lou Holtz once said,

"Show me someone who has done something worthwhile, and I will show you someone who has overcome adversity." I know I am that someone he speaks of. I believe that you are, too! The bigger your dreams are, the more difficult it will be to get where you are headed. Every adverse situation presents an opportunity, and you must be willing to find it, when times get rough. You must fully equip yourself to handle your business to the best of her ability.

Be True to You

Is there a part of you that you want everyone to see? Even if they just get a dose of who you truly are, would that make you feel more confident, freer, or truer to yourself? I ask this question because as I mature, I become truer to who I truly am. I am a chick from the hood, who happens to know how to adapt to all environments with ease. I still have desires to relate to my upbringing in a way that reflects that I have not forgotten where I've come from. I don't ever want to feel bad about what makes me feel good, but I realize that we can't let everyone know everything about us. However, we can show them who we truly are, when the moment is valuable.

About the Author

Serita Love, an Englewood native from Chicago, mom and self-professed "Success Junkie" educates, motivates and inspires by combining book and street smarts. She is a relational, group, and organizational professional who has a background that includes community outreach, public speaking, special events and integrated marketing communications. She has worked on countless experiential marketing and guerrilla marketing campaigns for many Fortune 500 Brands such as Starbuck's, P&G, and Safeway, Inc.

From losing her mom as a child to deciding to take her father off life support in 2017, Serita Love knows what it's like to overcome adversity. From being voted Most Likely to Succeed" in high school to being pregnant a year-and-a-half after high school, nothing stops her from achieving her life goals! Her efforts provide people hope to press forward. The Success Junkie brand poses as an antidote for success for many who are STUCK or under-inspired.

Serita gets her hands dirty as a talker and doer. From speaking and volunteering to donating to causes that promote upward social mobility, she is on a mission to get people hooked on ambition. She grew up seeing people hooked on negative habits. Her mission is simply to get people hooked on positive habits that are life-changing. She has worked with several organizations, such as the Chicago Urban League, Zillow Group, Junior Achievement Worldwide, the Chicago Public Schools, Rotary International, the Chicago Police Department, Alpha Kappa Alpha Sorority, Inc. and many more to be a solution to the problems around her, not just a witness.

Leadership became a staple in her life early on as a young girl in Englewood. As the author of *The Success High: 12 Steps to Getting and Staying Ahead*, Serita is branching out to spread her gospel for achievement. In her book, she highlights a positive First Hit, Side Effects to being Ambitious and Success Overdose.

Just like alcoholics have AA, Success Junkies have Serita Love. Many have a craving to achieve more. Success Junkies bring it to fruition. Serita is also a 40 Under 40 Young Women's Professional League award recipient, and one of *ChicagoNow*'s People & Organizations to Watch.

Visit www.SeritaLove.com or contact her at SeritaLove@gmail.com

Dr. Shirley Clark

Resetting Your Life for Success

If you live long enough, there will be many challenges you will encounter. As of this writing, I am 59 years old. When I look back over my life, I never would have thought I would have had to walk through all the things I had to face.

After being reared in gross poverty and overcoming this, I thought this was the biggest giant or adversity I would endure in my life. I remember as a youth living in such substandard conditions and desiring so much to have the American dream (a house, a car, money, a career, success, jewelry, clothes, etc.). Of course, during that time in my life, I did not know it was called the American Dream, but as I grew up and began to learn more about life and the systems of this world, I was introduced to this terminology.

I was in my mid-twenties when things truly began to change for me. By this time, I was a Christian and married. I cannot fully articulate to you the poverty mentality that I walked in. But my daily routine throughout my childhood and teenage years was about survival—what I was going to eat; what I was going to wear; where I was going to sleep, etc. My family endured an economic threat every day of my childhood life. Needless to say, my self-esteem was extremely low. As well, I could not pronounce words that began with the letter "S" like my name, Shirley. My mind was truly in a low place and I did not know how to get out of the situation. There was no frame of reference of escape for me!

Also, I did not know how to write a complete sentence. The only thing I could write was a run-on sentence. Reading, writing and arithmetic did not make sense to me. In fact, I saw no need for it because of the condition my family was living in. I could not see how learning to read, write or do math would keep our lights or water from being turned off. This was the way my mind processed going to school. So, I went to school because we were supposed to. I never fully understood why I had to go to school nor did my teachers reinforce the importance of education to ME other than the fact I needed to learn the information they were teaching and do the homework to pass the grade. Basically, I saw no way out of living the way we were living.

My mother had seven children and I was the youngest. She had a sixth grade education. All my siblings except the sister that is closest to my age dropped out of high school. Also, more than ninety-five percent of my extended relatives did not have degrees beyond a high school diploma within three generations. So, I definitely had no model, no frame of reference to change my situation. However, within me, I saw myself heading a business, sitting like a CEO at the head seat at a conference room table.

When I started working, one of the jobs I eventually landed was a substitute library assistant position. After working in this capacity for a few months, a full-time position opened up for the supervisor of the overdues department. I applied for it and was hired. I had no idea how I was being set up for greatness to be released in my life.

After working in this system for three years, my work environment became my classroom, my incubation center. It was in this place that the Dr. Shirley Clark that most people know today begin to emerge. Outside of prayer and my relationship with God, there is no other entity or person I would give homage to for my personal development than the library system. What happened? I had an aha moment to become a lifelong student.

I took advantage of the information hidden within the pages of the books that surrounded me every day. I began to check out twenty-five to thirty books at a time. I learned that I truly had to change what was in my head. And when I did, my world changed. I had to stop identifying with the pain of my past, but I also had to see my pain as life's lessons. What I learned was the lessons that I went through were the things God used to bring me to the place where I am now. It was about resetting my life for success and understanding that there were blessings in the lessons.

No matter what you have gone through in life (divorce, abuse, bankruptcy, failed business, miscarriage, sexual assault, bad credit, car accident, sickness, etc.), you can change the ending or outcome of your situation. This is what I did.

There are so many things I can additionally share regarding my journey to success, but I want to share just a few benchmarks you can use to reset your life for success regardless of where you are today.

1. **Conscious effort to change**

   Change will begin in your life when you become committed to the process. You have to do everything intentionally. Change will only happen when you make a conscious effort to choose a new way of doing things—new behaviors and habits have to be formed. Daily you must be intentional about your call to action steps to reinforce your new belief system. Every day you have to actively apply an opposing force to your current norm to activate your future norm. Every dream will require some type of sacrifice!

2. You have seeds of greatness within you

Inside every human being are seeds of greatness. It is what we do with these seeds that determines our outcome. When God created you, there was a prophetic destiny attached to your life. You have to learn or discover what God has called you to do, and when you do, do everything in your power to release that greatness. You have to prepare, position and persevere at all cost to release your greatness in life. This is not a "mother may I" time; it is taking hold of your destiny and calling in life to release it into your now.

We are the sum total of what we were birthed into and exposed to. Unfortunately, there were good and bad things and patterns we were exposed to that created the wrong image of who we really are. Therefore, we are now walking out these subconscious patterns and behaviors that were formed. But I have great news! You can change these paradigms. This is why we have to be intentional and committed to our change. Besides, we don't know what we don't know. I love what best-selling author Anik Singal says in his book, *Escape*, "If you want to create success, you first need to dissect your past, understand your current paradigms, and if necessary, map a course to change your paradigms." He goes on to say, "If your past paradigms are not in alignment with attracting success, you need to change them—there is no way around it." You cannot skip this process!

I have had to do this over and over in my life. As I made mistakes along my journey of success, I just said, "I won't do this again...another life lesson." Yes, some of these lessons have been tough, but God graced me to get through them. You can get through them as well! Press the reset button and decide you are going to reinvent your day; you are going to redesign your future. Thomas Jefferson, former president of the United States said, *"Nothing can stop the man with the right mental attitude from achieving his goal; nothing on earth can help the man with the wrong mental attitude."*

3. Learn to fail forward

Failing is not a crime! Failing is about you not quitting. Winners never quit! So, you have failed at something...so what? It does not mean you are a failure. Many people who have done great things in this world have fail numerous times before they got it right or convinced others to believe in their dream. The *Rocky* movie that Sylvester Stallone wrote was rejected more than 1,500 times, but he did not give up. Because he did not give up, there were four additional movies based on the first movie that grossed a total of over $115 million. It is also said that Walt Disney was turned down 302 times before finally getting financing for Walt Disney World. Likewise, the founder of Kentucky Fried Chicken, Colonel Sanders, was rejected 1,009 times before finding someone to accept his fried chicken recipe. You see, you must give yourself permission to fail and to excel. However, giving yourself permission to fail does not mean you are desiring to fall. It just means you are NOT going to allow a setback to knock you out of the game. You are going to see it as a lesson to move forward.

Lastly, you must stop giving your past too much energy. When you continuously rehearse your failures whether verbally or internally, you prolong the pain or moments associated with them. Therefore, you will never move forward in a *timely* manner. That which was a moment has become protracted. You must stop judging yourself through your pain and your past. As well, you have to shut everything else down around you (the Internet, family members, friends, colleagues, etc.) that reminds you of that pain.

4. **Increase your value and worth**

The quickest way to increase your value and worth is become a lifelong student. If you work a job, there are basically two reasons you were hired: for what you know and your skill-sets. If you want to make more money in life, you have to read more materials about wealth, finance and money. If you want to become a better salesman, read more books on how to sell. This is not rocket science. You get paid for what you know and your skill sets. Also, you can learn a new trade and become certified. Energy flows where energy grows. You have to activate your potential.

For me, this truly has been my path of success. When I learned something in a book or from an article, and it was something I could implement immediately, I did it. You have to be your own rescuer. It is about tapping into your God-given abilities, so that the universe will engage in your growth and elevation. It is giving God and the universe more to work with. It is called the "Law of Attraction." You attract what you are.

People who study successful people find that one of the most common traits among them is that they read a lot. For example:

- **Tony Robbins** – reads at least thirty minutes a day
- **Oprah Winfrey** – loves reading and chooses a book a month for her book club
- **Bill Gates** – reads a book a week
- **Mark Cuban** – reads more than three hours per day

If you want to be successful, I recommend you set aside some time every day to read something about success, money, wealth and finance. Don't forget you can also listen to audio books in your car while driving and you can take online courses. I did it all. Listen, what do you have to lose? Nothing. You have everything to gain.

Today, whatever you are going through, let it just be that—going through. Don't put stop signs where there should be yield signs. What you have gone through in your past should not be a fortress, but a platform. It is not about despite; it is because of. If you are still struggling to be successful in life, give yourself permission to move forward NOW. You can no longer afford to play the record of failure in your mind (and some of you have it on auto repeat) if you want to do great things in this earth. You have to look beyond your past to focus on your future. When I did this, my life changed drastically! According to Gil Penchina, "Momentum begets momentum, and the best way to start is to start."

About the Author

For over thirty-five years, Dr. Clark has served as a catalyst in the community to provoke people to fulfill their destiny in life. And because of Dr. Clark's passion for helping people to succeed, she has authored more than thirty inspirational, motivational and business books. Such books as *Pray & Grow Richer, Think Like A Millionaire, Be A Millionaire, Discovering Your Destiny, Empowered Overcomers, 18 Biggest Mistakes Most Self-Publishers Make, Daily Dose of Direction for Women in Business*, and her latest book, *7 Day Guide From Being An Employee To Becoming An Entrepreneur*.

However, Dr. Clark's life has not always mirrored this greatness. She was born and reared in poverty. Through much perseverance and prayer, Dr. Clark defied all the odds. A native of Washington, North Carolina, (known as Little Washington), Dr. Clark is no stranger to hard times and barrenness. Today, she is an international motivational conference speaker, a television/radio host, an award-winning #1 Amazon bestselling author, a digital educator and a marketplace leader.

Dr. Clark is a highly sought-out motivational keynote speaker, coach and trainer who has spoken to audiences from as few as twenty-five to as many as 30,000. As a speaker, Dr. Clark has shared the stage and been on programs with prominent speakers such as former Governor Rick Perry of Texas; Les Brown, master coach and world-renowned motivational speaker; Dr. Keith Johnson, America's #1 confidence coach; Lisa Nichols, world-renowned personal development coach and *New York Times* best-selling author; Dr. George Fraser, founder of the fifth largest business seminar in America; Bishop T. D. Jakes, former daytime television talk show host, movie producer and *New York Times* best-selling author; and Dr. Michael Roberts, one of the largest real estate and hotel owners in the United States and abroad.

Contact Dr. Shirley by mail to 4213 Peggy Lane, Plano, Texas 75074, by telephone 972-571-6234 or email Shirley@DrShirleyClark.org. Be sure to visit her website at www.DrShirleyClark.org.

Dr. Stan "Breakthrough" Harris

Worth of a Woman: From the Perspective of a Man Raised by a Mother/Grandmother, Married to a Woman, and Who Helped Birth a Daughter Who Are all Women of Worth!

This project and collaboration called *Women of Worth, an Anthology* just might be one of the most important things being done to help empower a generation of young women to know their worth. Dr. R.G. Lee, the great preacher of many years ago, who I enjoyed listening to in my teen years, often asked the question, which is also a profound and piercing statement: "Who can elevate a man than a woman of worthy purposes, but who can so degrade a man than a woman of unworthy purposes!" Dr. Lee was clear, after pastoring world-famous churches and traveling the globe preaching his famous sermon,

"Payday Someday," that a woman who knew her worth could be very detrimental, or more importantly, very instrumental to a man's success!

Years ago, a woman and her husband were returning from their 25th high school reunion when the husband blurted out, "Did you notice your old flame was in attendance and he is only a guy who drives a garbage truck? Aren't you so glad you married me, a bank president instead?" The woman smiled and responded, "Well baby, of course I'm glad I married you. But had I married him, he wouldn't be a garbage truck driver. He would have been a bank president instead!" This woman was clear about her value and didn't want her husband to misunderstand either!

In the beginning, God, the Creator created three distinct categories with very different purposes. First, He created Creation: the universe, sun, moon, stars, and earth, etc. The second thing He created were the Creatures, such as giraffes, elephants, monkeys, whales, insects, etc. Then He made his crowning creation that would be in His likeness and in His image. The third thing He made was a Cultivator and Co-Creator, mankind! Contrary to popular belief, we are not a higher form of animal. We have a soul and a spirit. We can think, reason and much more. We are not the result of a big bang! (by the way, if there was nothing in the beginning, what exploded? If there was nothing there, who lit the explosives?)

When you talk worth and esteem, I teach God-worth and God-esteem. Self-esteem and self-worth are based on self, which can be up when you do well and drop low when you mess up. But God-esteem and God-worth are based on an unchangeable God, so they never change! When you realize how special you are, that God spoke to make everything else, but when He made mankind (male and female), He used His very own hands. That makes you a masterpiece. You are a product of and possess a piece of the Master! Then our great God went a step further and breathed into man the breath of life. God was the first to give CPR! Do you realize that your form was fashioned by the Master and His breath is what you breathe? Truly you are somebody special; you have great worth! If no one else recognizes your worth, it does not diminish one iota who and whose you are! Remember, you are a masterpiece because you are a piece of and product of the Master! It would do you well to stop right here and write that out, but this time personalize it and read it aloud for the next twenty-one days while looking in the mirror! "_____, you, my sister, are a masterpiece because you are a product of and piece of the Master!"

Most of us have heard stories of paintings that went for outrageous amounts of money simply because of the fame of the one painting it. In 2015, a Picasso smashed the auction record when someone paid $172 million for his masterpiece, *Les femmes d'Alger*. When a famous artist such as Picasso, Van Gogh, Francis Bacon, Alice Neal, Faith Ringgold, Kara Walker or the like creates a work of art, the price or worth is increased. Well, they all pale in comparison to when the King of Glory puts His hands on His crowning creation—you!

When God made Adam, He also gave him an assignment to cultivate and co-create. He said that Adam needed help to carry out this daunting task and a helpmate would be arranged to assist and work alongside Adam. The incredible thing was that the help Adam needed was not something outside of him, but rather someone already inside of him! God becomes the first doctor, performs the first surgery, and says that this will be a painful process. So painful in fact that God put Adam into a deep sleep.

On a side note, some of my white classmates tried to tease me in college by saying, "Adam was a white man and we can prove it!" I disagreed but asked, "Why would you claim such a thing and how can you prove it?" They responded, "Adam was white because God took his rib. If he were black it could have never happened!" They were almost rolling on the floor laughing. I very calmly waited for them to chill a bit and then I replied, "I actually can prove that he was indeed black." They looked at me in shock and amazement and all of them said, "Wait, there is no way that you can prove that. We just lowered the hammer on you."

I proceeded to say, "I won't even use the fact that Eden was in Africa and the soil is very dark. I'm just going to use your own silly rationale against you and hang you on your own gallows like Haman." (Esther 7:10) I said, "God had to put Adam to sleep to get that rib from him!" Many of them fell on the ground laughing and they also responded,

"You got us really good, Harris, that was a classic answer. You shut all of us up for good!"

Allow me to use my sanctified imagination for a minute. I can see in my mind's eye, as Adam starts dreaming of the help God was going to make for him. Adam had seen all the animals, and in fact named them all without the help of a computer, Google or a dictionary (imagine that). But Adam's best dream of a helpmate fell very short because when he awoke to God's final touch, Adam exclaimed, "Wow, Wooo Man or Womb-man" or as we say woman. I mean Adam probably said, "my dream was good, but I woke up and it wasn't a nightmare, but rather far better than I could have ever imagined!"

He said something like this, "What a masterpiece, that has a womb for my seed to connect with, and we together will co-create other masterpieces!" Long before the first man ever entered the sacred garden of the woman (after marrying her), the woman was already in the secret place (rib) of the man! (You might need to read that one again and tweet that!)

By the way men, she came from inside Adams rib, which is the closest thing to his heart, to be beside him. Not from his feet to be trampled upon, or his head to lead him, nor his backside to be sat upon! Now if I said this at church, I could hear all the awesome women shouting "AMEN, please say that again Doc!" This is a book so let me say it to myself, by myself "Amen Doc!"

Let's return to the theme of the book. I submit to you that when women understand their worth, they become like my mom, Thelma, and grandmom Daisy (both R.I.P), my wife Nadia, and my daughter Christina. All have had and have a profound effect on my life and the people around them. Women who understand their worth and rise up to be the queens God made them to be often have three distinct things that result when it comes to their men: 1) they become King Manifesters; 2) King Multipliers; and 3) King Makers!

My lovely mom realized her worth (although my dad didn't recognize his) and she raised five boys for most of her life before eventually marrying my stepdad. Always remember that when you don't know the worth, value or use of a thing, you tend to misuse or abuse it. I believe many women today are not just abusing themselves but allowing others to abuse them because they haven't been taught their proper value or worth. It's so bad that some are comfortable with abuse and get uncomfortable and suspicious when someone tries to treat them with the due respect, value, and worth that are rightfully theirs.

My mom could have lived on welfare but instead started working and got a second job to make ends meet. She had dignity and self-respect, and even though we were poor she believed in taking her responsibilities seriously. By the way, the word "responsibility" broken down literally means respond-with-ability.

I'll never forget when my mom and grandmother Daisy would speak life into me. Many years after graduating at the top of my high school class, as well as graduating college (Who's Who in American College and Universities), traveling all over the world preaching and teaching, my mom said, "Son, I'm honored just to know a man of your stature." I responded, "Mom, thanks but you are seeing the harvest of the seeds you sowed many years ago." Once when I was breaking a stack of thirteen bricks on fire, my mom said, "Son, are you going to break them with your head?" I said, "No ma'am, just my hand this time!" You see my mom and grandmother's example, their belief in me, tied with their words spoken to or about me, made me into a king! My grandmother's prayers and teaching me the scriptures when I was a child help set me apart. You see when a woman knows her worth, she becomes a King Maker.

When I met Nadia many years ago, whom I refer to as my A.B.C.D. (Adorable Brown Carmel Delight) and (Angelic Blessed Chocolate Delicacy), I was so impressed that she knew her worth as a woman and carried herself with dignity and class. She's by far the nicest person that I've ever met, friendly and beautiful beyond measure! She is one hundred times more beautiful on the inside than the outside and believe me when I say she is smoking hot on the outside. Once while traveling we stopped at a hotel and there was a sign that read "No Smoking." I said, "I guess my wife can't come in." The clerk behind the desk asked, "Does your wife smoke?" I responded, "No ma'am, she doesn't smoke, but she is definitely smoking!" The clerk replied, "Well Dr. Harris, we will make an exception for her in that case. By all means bring her in!"

Nadia brings out the best in me, and from the time we got married she started referring to me as her king. That made me feel a little uncomfortable and uneasy at first, but I soon got used to it and of course I started calling her my queen. Later I realized she knew her worth all along and actually helped me increase in my knowledge of my own! She was a single woman who manifested the king she had been preparing for! Ladies, when you walk in the awareness of your worth, you will become a King Manifester. Sooner or later, your Boaz will find you! I told Nadia when I met her that there was something about her essence that makes me want to be more, do more and accomplish more. She's a King Multiplier!

My daughter, Christina Nicole Harris, now a professor at Temple University while finishing a doctoral program in African Studies, has traveled to more than twenty-six countries to date. She is also a powerful young woman who knows her worth and makes me feel like I am invincible and able to leap tall buildings in a single bound. She has had to put many a want-to-be, make believe king-jokers in their place politely as she prepares for her Boaz. She also is so attractive, smart, brilliant, well versed and read. But most importantly, her Mom and I instilled in her a sense of her own worth and now she affects many others. I simply want to say to everyone reading this to know your worth so you can walk worthy. It's not easy, but it sure is worth it. The world and the best version of yourself is counting on you!

About the Author

Dr. Stan Harris is an evangelist, business and success coach, 10th degree black belt, author, master motivator and mentor to thousands. He has dedicated his life to empowering, educating, and elevating people to break through any barrier that would hinder their success by empowering them to become the best or at least a better version of themselves. He and Nadia say they are a covenant couple, building covenant relationships, based on the covenant of promise and they aspire to inspire breakthroughs even after they've expired. Be sure to visit www.DrBreakthrough.com or call (717) 275-3508.

Dr. Tonja Annette Gardner

A Mother of Worth

Growing up in Lake Providence, Louisiana, I had strong females in my family. My mom, Vanilla Closure, my aunt, Vernie Hawkins, and my grandmother, Mrs. Della Kelly Threats. I was always told that I could be whatever I wanted to be. Even through my high school years, the guidance and education I received was among the best and the positive reinforcement of my teachers, band leaders, cheer coach, Sunday School teachers, and family and friends was more than enough to make me understand that it didn't matter where I came from. I could go anywhere and be anything.

By the time I went to Grambling State University (GSU), I already struggled with self-esteem issues due to the dark tone of my skin. At GSU, I was made to feel like a beauty queen. I learned to love my skin tone and color and it made me feel strong and vibrant. I needed that strong and vibrant feeling because I was an accounting major and received a "D" in my first accounting course. I decided to talk to my accounting advisor, and he proceeded to tell me that maybe accounting was not for me. He continued by saying that maybe I should change my major to management, marketing or something.

Coupled with the difficulties of classes, I was in a very arduous relationship. At first, our relationship was like the best love story of all time. We spent so much time together and we were inseparable. He was so handsome and everyone around town loved him. He was also very popular, smart, and kind. But soon, our relationship turned physically violent. I would try to fight back, but he was much stronger than I was. Eventually, I would end up missing classes because my face was badly bruised. This eventually crippled my determination and made it very hard to make good grades; however, I was determined.

By the time I graduated from college, I had accepted my first job and before long, I was pregnant with our daughter. This was scary, yet exciting to me because my dream was to become a great mom and a beloved wife. My relationship had not improved and although I was carrying his child, the abuse continued. Yet, I was so determined to be a family, and not another statistic, I stayed in the relationship. As the abuse and ups and downs continued, I bore our son.

After my second child, we decided to give it another try, but the physical abuse continued. Once, when our son was an infant and our daughter was only three years old, he was physically abusing me and pushed me in the empty bathtub. Our daughter was screaming and telling him to stop hitting her mom. She was so afraid and visibly upset. I remember the look in my daughters' eyes. At that point I decided I did not want my daughter to grow up thinking it was okay for a man to physically abuse her. More importantly, because I had a son, I did not want him to grow up thinking that behavior was okay.

As I rose from the floor, wiped my face, and dusted off my clothes, I glanced at myself in the mirror. At first, I just looked off because I was sad, confused, hurt, and literally disgusted with myself for allowing the abuse to go on for so long. But then I looked again and this time, I decided to take a long look. I stared into my own eyes. Seconds, turned to minutes and before I knew it, the minutes had turned into an hour. I stared at myself, as if I was starring deep into my soul. And that is when my spirit knew, I was done! At that point, I ended an almost ten-year relationship.

Life was hard as a single mom with two small kids. Work was demanding and often caused me to have to make a choice between being a mom and an employee. Due to the complicated role of single mom with babies with severe asthma, I worked for several companies throughout my career. With each move came career elevation and a higher salary. Therefore, I am so thankful to my heavenly Father and my Lord and Savior Jesus Christ for always keeping me and my babies through good times and tough times.

As time went on, there was a handsome man dropping off a coworker in my apartment complex. I just happened to be outside with my kids while my daughter rode her bike in the common area. He saw me and decided to introduce himself, which led to us talking for the rest of the afternoon. He was nice and seemed like a natural with children. We laughed and talked each day afterwards. As the weeks passed, he asked if we could date and this began a short courtship between the two of us. I did not feel as if I was a woman worth a man's pride and joy, since I already had two children by a man who was no longer in my life, so I figured, well at least he is not beating on me. Within the year, we were married and shortly thereafter, we had our son. We were so happy and finally I had a real family and my children had a father.

We had some good years and some not so good. After my third child, I began to gain weight and he started to stray away and talk to other women. He started comparing me to the other women and I began to feel unloved and unappreciated, yet I was determined to stay in the marriage. We attended church often, although he was not a Christian. I remember a few years into the marriage, we attended the very first MegaFest in Atlanta, Georgia. During the Fest, I was engulfed in much needed prayer and supplication. I remember the lady pastor saying, "Before you go in to your house when you get home, say to God, get the devil out of my house." So, when we returned home, I stopped at the door and before we all went inside, I put both hands of the door and said, "God, get the devil out of my house."

Within the week, I found out that my husband was doing the unthinkable. He was demonstrating inappropriate behavior around my daughter. After I confronted him, he quickly fled the country and I was granted a divorce by default the following year. With this brutal discovery, I went into a silent depression. I felt like a failure. The most important things in the world to me were my kids and I felt like I had let them down by making a terrible decision to bring this person into their lives. I felt I had let my daughter down and I did not protect her from harm as I should have.

After this, I felt like I could not trust anyone. I was done with men and I would not trust another man around my daughter. I continued to live in the shadows for the next two years. Life had brought me down to my knees. I prayed and cried countless nights alone after I put my kids to bed. I didn't understand how God could allow this to happen to me. I felt with my first relationship, he tried to beat it out of me, but this time the hurt broke my spirit. My hopes were drenched in pain and I lost all self-esteem. I went to work, came home, and after helping my kids with homework, and making sure they were fed and bathed, I cried myself to sleep at night. I struggled to understand why my life had gone so wrong, while I prayed to God for wisdom and strength just to get through another day.

My dream of being a wife and a great mother was shattered. My ex-husband once told me that no other man was going to want me with three kids. That statement was etched in my mind and I believed him. I didn't even trust my own judgement and therefore, did not even entertain the thought of bringing anyone else into our lives. Besides, I would always remember what he said: You have three kids and no other man is going to want that package deal.

The kids and I continued to go to church every Sunday. I wanted to make sure they had a good Bible base just like I did growing up back home. While listening to the sermons, my pastor really spoke like he was eavesdropping on the conversations and prayers I had with the Lord the previous week. It was almost scary, uncanny and at the same time, it was amazing. I knew God still loved us and although I was depressed, I know it was God and the smiles of my babies that gave me the strength to get out of bed each morning and make it through the day. One Sunday, I decided to sit in the first few rows during service and my pastor looked straight at me and said, "These enemies that you see today, you shall see them again no more." Those words brought a peace over me that surpassed all understanding. Each week I went to church, God spoke to me through my pastor, and each time I became stronger and stronger in my faith.

In the next couple of years, we moved to a new home and school, and the children thrived in their new environment. My kids were ages six, eight, and twelve when they started their new schools. Life was finally beginning to make sense again. I was content. Me and my three! My daughter and I went to counseling and our relationship became stronger than ever. My life was centered around my children and their activities. The boys were in football and my daughter was a cheerleader. They had practice in the evenings after school and games on Saturdays. Sometimes my entire Saturday was spent at three football games. My children were happy and so was I. I even decided to occupy my mind and my nights by studying to earn a master's degree. Besides, I knew it would be a step in the right direction for my career path. Dallas Baptist University was a great choice and I knew I would increase my knowledge in my field, while also increasing my faith.

As the years passed, I knew I did not want my kids to think that love didn't exist, and I knew it had been a while since I even entertained the thought of being with a man, so I started dating again. Of course, I didn't take anyone too seriously because my priority was my children and I refused to allow them to be hurt again. Then, one Thanksgiving weekend, in an effort to find entertainment for my family, we went to a dance club in Dallas. For most of the night, I watched purses while my sisters danced, but then this wonderfully, handsome man with a distinctive accent asked me to dance. After we danced to the first song, we ended up dancing together for the rest of the night. I was in awe. During the course of the next few weeks, we would talk on the phone for hours. I remember when the kids and I went home for Christmas break, my parents wondered who I was on the phone with giggling for hours. He was articulate and brilliant. He was intelligent and didn't seem to be scared off when I told him I had three children. On New Year's Day of the next year, he played his guitar and sang to me. It was as if I was in heaven. Over the course of the months we dated, he invited me over to his place for. He was an amazing cook.

When he finally met my kids, he was automatically drawn to them. Within the first month of spending very little time with them, he had already learned their three distinct personalities. Over the next few months, as we got to know each other, I told him about my last marriage and what my daughter had been through. He was very sympathetic and expressed how sorry he was that we had to endure this pain. Months turned to years and my family and I became very comfortable with him. My daughter and I were very close, so we would talk all the time, and she assured me that she was very comfortable with him as well. After dating for five years, he asked me to marry him, and I said yes.

During our marriage, I went back to school and earned a Doctorate of Business Administration degree with a concentration in accounting. Oh yes, my Bachelor of Science degree from Grambling State University is in accounting as well. I also earned a Master of Business Administration degree with a concentration in accounting and a concentration in management. My life took an exhilarating turn for the better and if someone were to ask me how I made it through, I would tell them it was the blessings and grace of God.

Throughout my healing process, I understood that God will not let us be deceived. Even if you make a wrong decision, our Father in heaven will not let you stay in clutches of that bad decision. He is merciful and He will turn your life around if you believe and trust Him. I learned to appreciate the people in my life who loved me and whom I loved. I also learned to see the positive in every situation because things could always be worse. Negativity takes you down a path of despair, but positivity and trust in God will take you places you never dreamed possible.

My children are now young adults with careers, and I am still happily married to my dance partner and my love, Dr. Brian Inskip Gardner.

About the Author

Dr. Tonja Gardner is a business research scientist, a professor of accounting and management, an author, an entrepreneur, a conference speaker, trainer, a mother, and a wife. Dr. Gardner is the CEO of Genuine Accounting Services PLLC which provides accounting and tax services. She also volunteers at (WiNGS) Women in Need of Generous Support, in Dallas, Texas, where she teaches accounting and business strategies for aspiring entrepreneurs and is a member of God Leading Ladies at her local church. She works closely with the Wright Resource Group in Dallas to provide professional and leadership training for businesses and corporations.

Dr. Gardner furthered her education in accounting to encourage high school and graduate students to pursue a career in accounting. Her passion is educating students and business professionals on the importance of soft skills and the effects soft skills have on accomplishing their career goals.

To book Dr. Tonja Gardner to be a speaker or trainer at your next conference or event, email her at Tonja.Gardner@msn.com or visit her website at www.genuineaccountingservices.com. Dr. Tonja may also be reached at (214) 966-7575.

Ty Gray-El

A Black Woman's Smile

Do you know how strong you have to be to make a black woman smile?

Do you have any idea what an accomplishment that is?

She has borne the weight of this country on her back for 400 years.

She's been carrying the load of America in her belly since its infancy.

She has suffered the agony of unassisted, husband-less child-rearing since the 1600s.

Have you any idea how much strength it takes to put a smile on her face?

You need the strength of Sampson, the nerve of Joshua and the courage of David facing Goliath.

Cause she has cultivated in her womb the marvel of the universe, only to have her hopes and dreams aborted and her aspirations show up dead on arrival.

She's given birth to kings and queens and delivered on her majestic promise, only to have her children kidnapped and sold to a criminal with no respect for her royalty.

If you can make a black woman smile, you are a miracle worker.

Imagine breastfeeding your child in Virginia and having him snatched from your arms, branded; hijacked to Louisiana and publicly fondled on a New Orleans auction block.

If the memory of that pain was locked-bound in your DNA, would you be smiling?

If you breast-fed someone else's child only to watch her grow old enough to call you darky, pickaninny and nappy-headed Jigaboo, you wouldn't be smiling either.

If you can make a black woman smile you have DONE something.

If you can make her smile you, you are stronger than Atlas, cause God knows she has been.

She's been raped, ravaged and scorned...

and nearly annihilated.

She's been pimped, pummeled and stoned...

and deliberately depreciated.

She has cooked and cleaned and sewn…

and never been compensated.

She's been forced to watch the offspring of her loins mangled and maligned across centuries.

Her character has been continuously smeared; assassinated over and over and over,

again and again and again.

You ever thought about how strong you have to be, just to BE a black woman?

She's had to make brick without straw, after being

stripped of all her customs, all her culture and all her traditions.

No other woman in the history of the civilized world has gone through what she's gone through.

No other beings on the planet have endured what she has endured.

She's been chastised, criticized, demonized and terrorized.

She's had to stand when her man was bull-whipped for trying to stand.

She's had to stand when her man was castrated for trying to stand.

She's had to stand when her man was hung by his neck for trying to stand.

She's had to carry her man, cause every time he tried to carry himself, he was murdered for trying to do so.

Ask Betty Shabazz about Malcolm; ask Coretta Scott King about Martin;

ask Emmett Till's mother; ask Trayvon Martin's mother.

If you can make a black woman smile you have achieved something.

Since 1619 when we came in chains,

the entire world's been messing with her brain,

disrespecting her, calling her out of her name,

and she's tired...just plain Fanny Lou Hamer, tired...

Tired of being called B-words, and H-words and N-words and other-words and everything except the child of God that she is.

But...the one thing in this world that will make a black woman smile...is her man...

A real man!

If you're doing what you're supposed to do...she will smile...she will smile regularly and gladly.

So... man up my brother...

Man up and make your woman smile.

Treat her like the Queen that she is...

She deserves it...

And recognize this...

In all of God's Creation there is nothing more alluring, more appealing, or attractive; nothing more beautiful, nothing more charming, more charismatic, or captivating; nothing more delightful, nothing more elegant or exquisite; nothing more fascinating, nothing more gorgeous, nothing more inspiring, more intoxicating or invigorating; nothing more magnificent, there is nothing more lovely than a Black Woman's Smile.

"One Woman"

If one woman made up her mind

To everyone she meets, be kind

And fix her heart on that which is true

If one woman would be so bold

As to embrace the Gospel and hold

Just think what a million women could do

If one woman changed her thought

Each time the tempter brought

Some selfish scheme that would her neighbor undo

If she thought for just a minute

Just where is the kindness in it

Just think what a million thoughts like that could do

If Sarah could wait all those years

And God dried her barren tears

And widow Naomi's tears dried too

If Naomi could depend on Ruth

To faithfully tell her the truth

Just think what a million Ruth's could do

If Esther could find good reason

To stay patient throughout her season

And Bathsheba is how Solomon came through

If Deborah the prophetess judge

Could face enemies and not budge

Just think what a million Deborah's could do

If cousins Elizabeth and Mary

Could each miraculously carry

Both John and Savior Jesus too

If Martha's belief in what Jesus said

Raised Lazarus from his death-bed

Just think what a million Martha's could do

If one woman would take a second

When her needy neighbor beckoned

And followed literally Moses tenth command

With spirits filled and nourished

Our neighborhoods would flourish

How quickly peace would spread throughout this land

If one woman made up her mind

To no matter what, be kind

No matter what others might put her through

The strength of that woman's resolve

Would all our problems solve

And just think what a million women like that can do

About the Author

Ty Gray-EL is known as the Minister of Poetry. He is an internationally renowned storyteller and the founder of Breath of My Ancestors; a Cultural Enrichment Ministry. Ty earned a B.S. in Street-ology from the District of Columbia, a Master's Degree in Survival in the Ghettos of North America and a Ph.D. in Psyche-ology from the University of Hard Knocks. While some laugh at Ty's academic achievements, because he was once labeled uneducable, he is as proud of his accomplishments as anyone holding degrees from Howard, Harvard or Yale. He is an author, activist, poet, playwright, public speaker, husband, proud father of four and Minister at New Revival Kingdom Church.

Contact Ty at his website www.tygrayel.com and follow him on Facebook @tygrayel.

Wendala "Wendy" Bradley

5Define Your Shine

There is a shine determined to materialize within all of us that is often dimmed by the pain, hurt, and turmoil of life's experiences. Until we acknowledge our hurts, the shine that is desperately waiting to beam, will remain dimmed. However, once we acknowledge and understand the source and root cause of the shine dimmer, it will then be defined. For years, what I thought was the source of my pain, my main shine dimmer, actually was not.

I can remember it as though it happened yesterday. The phone call, the news from the doctor, the drive to the hospital—only to find that by the time we got there, she was no longer with us. She was my mom. My mom was an incredible God-fearing woman who brought her children up in the church, taught us how to survive, taught us about the value of a dollar, and how to take nothing, make something out of it and sell it! Yep, she knew how to squeeze a penny, as they use to say. Being the youngest of four children, and the only girl, my mom and I had a very special bond and close relationship. We talked but not necessarily about life, just about whatever was to be discussed at the moment. Spoiled you say?? Cherished I'd say!

Now, while I had chores and rules, I can say I got away with a lot more than my brothers. Okay, it was close to getting away with murder. Well, all that "cherished life" disappeared the day she died. It was one of the hardest challenges I had to endure at the time. It was tough enough to not only know that my mother, my confidant, and my comforter, would no longer be here for me but I was also only sixteen years old. For most, that was the age where you started to learn about life, or at least as much as you would allow someone to teach you. But for me, it was the beginning of what felt like the end. There were a lot of facts about life that I didn't know or had the opportunity yet to ask. Who was going to teach me? Who was going to be there for me? Who would guide me through the pains of life? How would I survive without her? These were questions that were left unanswered and I ultimately had to learn on my own and as they say, the hard way.

Now, my father was there and he wasn't just there, at the same time. He served on the board of directors of the hospital my mother died. Hands on, at home dad, there every day, but still a million miles away from raising his daughter. The pain of my mother's death was one that could not surpass any other (so I thought), as this was the first of what was to be many shine dimmers in my life.

My mother had been in and out of the hospital many times for several years after I was born, however, through all the pain and suffering, she never once made it feel as though being a mom was a burden. During one of the visits right before she died, she said she wanted me to live with my aunt because "I needed to be raised by a woman." I didn't realize what she actually meant was she knew my father wasn't going to be there for me as she had been, but I didn't listen. I knew my aunt was strict and we didn't have the closest relationship so, like any other hard-headed teenager, I decided to be grown, make my own decisions, and instead of fulfilling my mother's deathbed wish, I stayed with my dad. Well, little did I know that would be another beginning to, what felt like, another ending in my life. One day, I heard my dad talking to my aunt on the phone saying, "You need to come and get your niece because I don't have time to raise no girl." Those words pierced through my heart like a hot knife cutting through butter. All I could think of at the time was why would he say that? Why would he call my aunt to come and get me? Did he not love me anymore? Did he really not want me around anymore? Why??

I was emotionally shattered by the very person I thought would be my protector. My sense of belonging was snatched away from me by the very person I needed, wanted, and expected stability from, especially now. How could he say that he didn't have time for me? I was his baby girl. I was the cherished one. I was the youngest and the one who needed love and compassion the most. Instead, I felt as though he just threw me into the arms of someone else to care for me. Although this left me feeling very unwanted, unloved and betrayed, I still treated him with love and respect as he was still my father. Shortly after that call I moved in with my mother's twin sister and her family, who became my guardian as I was still considered a minor. It was very hard for me because I knew that I wouldn't like living with her. Not because she didn't love me —she did. But because I knew that she would be A LOT tougher on me than my mother had been and that is not what I wanted or needed at this particular time. What a dimmer!

Not getting the love and attention I was accustomed to made living with my aunt very challenging. She loved me but it was more of a tough love compared to my mother's. I didn't make it easy on her either because I knew I didn't want to be there, and I was still hurting. Not only had I just lost my mother, but I concluded in my mind that my father didn't want me around anymore. My oldest brother who I could have lived with didn't take me in and the rest of my brothers (all older) went on about their lives.

I was in pain and confused and in my mind, I thought my aunt would have embraced me with love and tenderness, or at least compassion. I thought I would still get that "cherished" treatment, but I didn't. At times, I felt I was being punished for not having a mother any longer and once again, I was left to conclude in my mind, that I was unwanted and unloved. Yes, this was yet another shine dimmer in my life. Needless to say, I do know her intentions were well, and she was being the best person she could be.

Not long after I moved in, my aunt became very ill and like my mom, she was also in and out of the hospital. They both had been diagnosed with lupus in the years prior. It didn't affect my aunt as severely as it had my mother as the effects of lupus came later for her. Eventually, my aunt was admitted to the hospital, had several surgeries. The day she told me she wanted me to "always take care of myself" and "that she really did love me" was the last day I saw her alive.

Although our relationship had turbulence, she was still the only mother I had and like her twin, my mom, I had to watch her die each day I was with her. Once again, I was faced with the uncertainty of how I could go on without guidance and without a mother figure. Who would be there for me now? Yes, my uncle was there and was nice. He didn't talk much but I always knew he cared about me, however, he wasn't my mother, my aunt, my brothers, or my father. Sure, I was eighteen now but I still felt lost, confused, and once again alone and unwanted. I felt I had no one to turn to, talk to, to console me. There was no one to care for or about me or to care about how I felt or what I was going through.

Not having anyone in my life to guide me along the way left me feeling unloved, not cherished, and invaluable. This was yet again, another shine dimmer.

During the time of my aunt's death, I began, what I thought, was a serious relationship. Of course, without guidance and having been through the recent losses, I flew right into it with full force. I didn't realize I was looking for someone to fill all the holes that were left behind from the blasts of losses and rejection I endured. He of course painted the pretty picture of someone who genuinely cared. Well, it wasn't too much longer that I found myself pregnant with his child. That pretty picture soon started looking very ugly.

I attended the doctor visits—alone. I received no help from him so, I was left alone to care for myself and my unborn child. My emotions were once again shattered by a man I thought would be there for me, care for me, and protect me. Instead, I was left feeling alone, unloved, and rejected once again. I was living away from home in a different state at the time and since it was becoming difficult for me emotionally and financially, I decided to move back home. As time progressed, it came closer to the delivery date of the baby. As I was sleeping one night, my mother appeared in my dreams. In the dream, she sat next to my hospital bed saying, "Don't worry, everything will be alright, and you will be okay." Incidentally, she appeared in my dreams twice more with the same message. I would soon come to find out why.

I only had a couple weeks left when I started feeling pains. As the nurse checked me, she didn't hear a heartbeat. She called the doctor in and again there was no heartbeat. He explained, "Sometimes it's an equipment error. We are going to send you to the hospital to have an internal x-ray." At the hospital, the specialist checked and once again there was no heartbeat. Then, they made the official statement: "She's not alive." My baby girl was gone. I was devastated! Not only was she gone, but I still had to deliver her. I wanted them to give me a C-section or something because I had to endure the pain of her death and the pain of her delivery all at once. Of course, they said that I had to go through with it and at the age of nineteen, without my mother, my aunt, or the father of my baby there to comfort me, I experienced a stillbirth— alone.

Later, I had the aha moment and the dreams became very clear to me. Wow! My mother appeared in my dreams to comfort me. She came to assure me I would be okay. Within the last three years, I had lost her, felt rejected by my father, and my aunt passed away. Now my unborn child was gone, too. Once again, my emotional stability was shattered with yet another shine dimmer.

It was once said that a woman's worth is intrinsic. If my worth is said to be intrinsic, it means there is a sense of belonging. If lacked emotional stability from the very people who were to care for me, and my sense of belonging was obsolete, then what is my sense of belonging?? You cannot have a sense of belonging if you do not feel as though you belonged. After my mother's death, I needed to belong, and I felt I didn't. I needed to be protected, and I felt I wasn't. I needed to feel loved, and I felt I was unloved.

While I realized no one could replace the love of my mother, I thought I would have felt more love than I did. I needed to know that despite what happened, I was still wanted, especially being the only girl and youngest child. This was supposed to be the time in my life where my worth should have been shaped and molded into something strong by the people who were caring for me. Instead, little by little, it was torn to pieces.

Due to the lack of knowing my worth, my life's winding road began to be filled with unhealthy relationships. I eventually married and had four beautiful children, however, the marriage slowly started fading away. What I didn't realize was that the holes left behind from the past hurts and losses in my life were still open and the man I married couldn't fill them – no man could. Those holes, as I learned later in life, could only be filled by the love of Jesus Christ. Although the marriage ended, my desire to live and not die, succeed and not fail, did not.

Despite all the holes left behind from the rejection, deaths, additional unhealthy relationships and shattered emotional stability, I chose to keep my head up and move forward as I was now a single mom of four little ones. Heck, with four children, I was even denied public assistance and that's what made me dig my heels in and push forward. I became unstoppable and did whatever it took to take care of my children, without assistance or help from anyone. I immediately went into survival mode. I moved to different states within the federal government for promotion purposes. I worked hard and in addition to my government job, I worked second jobs on the weekends and sometimes even a third at night during the week just to make ends come closer because they never did meet. Hee!

Now, I can say that by God's grace, I have arrived. I quickly moved up the federal government career ladder, which allowed for a more comfortable life for me and my children. All four of my children are now grown, very successful, and living their own lives; some have even begun their own families. In addition, I currently own a decorating business and I'm in the process of forming an organization that will help, encourage, and empower single moms.

A few years ago, I attended a table talk session given by my pastor. Another member of the session began discussing the rejection in her life. As I listened, she said things that sounded very familiar to me. Rejection!!! It was then I realized that all these years what I thought was the main source of my pain, my main shine dimmer—the deaths in which I endured—were not dimmers at all. Yes, they were contributors, especially not having my mother around, but it was not the main shine dimmer. Rejection was the real root of my hurt. Rejection was my biggest shine dimmer! And I realized it began with my father, the one very person I desired to help me heal.

That was a true defining moment for me. It was when I defined my shine! In doing so, I have now defined who I am *not*. I am *not* unwanted, I am *not* unloved, and I am *not* alone. Defining who I am *not,* helped me know, trust and believe, the true definition of who I *am*. I *am* wanted, I *am* loved, I *am* victorious, and I *am* a wonderful work of God!

While your shine may be dimmed
By life's turmoil and distress
In time it will illuminate
By God's grace and your finesse

You are an integral part
Of God's glorious plan
So do not allow your shine to be darkened
By the words or actions of any woman or man

Once the root of your pain
In which you have endured
Are realized and acknowledged
The main shine dimmer will be understood

So Define Your Shine
Let God's inner light beam
For you are not a victim of your circumstances
But a beautiful reflection of who God designed you to be!

Matthew 5:14; 16 says "You are the light of the world." "Let your light shine before others." Life's pain is a part of life's gain. No matter how grim we see the hurt and disappointments, they are the elements and ingredients of the Potter's clay that makes us who we are. Understanding that puts the shimmer and glimmer on the dimmer. So, no matter what, my shine will continue to illuminate before others as I understand and have acknowledged the root of my pain and have therefore, Defined My Shine, and so can you!

About the Author

Wendala (Wendy) Welch Bradley was raised in Peoria, Illinois. She met some of life's hardest challenges and decided early in life not to allow those challenges to dictate who she was going to be. Some of the challenges she endured were hard to accept but she did so despite her circumstances.

Wendala desires to help as many women as possible to see that no matter how much "stuff" we have endured, there is a special diamond quality deep within all of us that is eagerly waiting to emerge and shine. Through that desire, Wendala started an organization for single moms and is the founding president of Single Moms Ambitiously Rising Together (S.M.A.R.T.), which was birthed out of the need to empower, enrich, encourage, and enhance the lives of the single mom by ministering, teaching, educating, and providing resources.

Wendala is also an owner of SimpliExquisite Event Designs, an event decorating business. She is also an author and the CEO of her life. For more information or to schedule a speaking engagement, contact Wendy at wen.roch4@gmail.com or smartsinglemoms@gmail.com.

Other books published by FIG Publishing & Dr. Katrina Ferguson

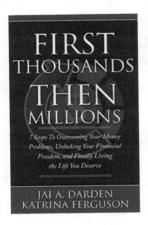

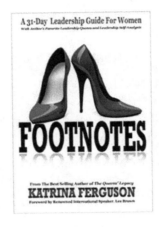

FOR YOUR
NEXT EVENT
BOOK

Dr. Katrina Ferguson

...XECUTIVE INFLUENCER
...SPIRATIONAL SPEAKER
...RSONAL DEVELOPMENT
...ST-SELLING AUTHOR
...ADERSHIP TRAINER
...ANSFORMATION COACH

@DrKatrinaSpeaks
Katrina@KatrinaFerguson.com
#DrKatrinaSpeaks
703.906.1711

DR. KATRINA FERGUSON

KATRINAFERGUSON.COM

A PROUD SPONSOR OF
#WOWMOVEMENT

SHOP FREEMART

PRESENTS

HYDRATION DROPS

OVER 75% OF AMERICANS ARE CHRONICALLY DEHYDRATED YET IT SEEMS THAT EVERYONE IS CARRYING AROUND BOTTLES OF WATER. ACTUALLY DRINKING WATER IS IMPORTANT. STAYING HYDRATED IS IMPERATIVE.

Drinking the right kind of water is one of your best natural protections against all kinds of diseases. If the body's cells become dehydrated, they shrivel up, making it easy for viruses and diseases to attack.

Water is a vital component of all bodily fluids, tissues, cells, lymph, blood and hormones and the mucous membranes need plenty of water to keep them soft and free from friction on their delicate surfaces.

DEHYDRATION can lead to DEFICIENCY which can lead to DYSFUNCTION which can ultimately lead to DEATH.

VISIT WWW.200DISEASES.COM TO SEE MORE OF THE BENEFITS OF DRINKING THE RIGHT KIND OF WATER

GET YOUR FREE MEMBERSHIP AND ORDER YOUR HYDRATION DROPS TODAY!

WOWDROPS.ORG
FOR MORE INFORMATION

CPSIA information can be obtained
at www.ICGtesting.com
Printed in the USA
FFHW012310300419
52080704-57529FF

9 780998 169019